An Autobiography by

BARRY SANDERS

His Story in His Own Words,
Written With Mark E. McCormick

Mission Matters   Mr. Century City, LLC

Edited and Updated with New Content 2023

For information, visit www.barrysanders.com

Originally published by Clerisy Press, Emmis Books, December 10, 2003.

Published by Mission Matters and Mr. Century City, LLC

For information, visit www.MissionMatters.com

The Mr. Century City Logo is a trademark of Mr. Century City, LLC.
Mission Matters, Beverly Hills, CA

Managing Editor:
Adam Torres / @AskAdamTorres

Editor:
Hillary Crawford

Beverly Hills, CA 90212
www.MissionMatters.com

Let's Connect

E-book ISBN 13: 978-1-949680-50-8

Paperback ISBN 13: 978-1-949680-51-5

Hardcover ISBN 13: 978-1-949680-52-2

Barry's Impact

"When you're trying to stop him, you surround him, you try to contain him. You're also trying not to make the ESPN highlights with him faking you out of your shoes. I remember on one play, they threw a flare pass to the side of the field, and I came running up on him."

— Louis Oliver, former NFL Miami Dolphins Safety

"I've never seen anyone, or played against anyone, who was like him. He defied all the rules of tackling. Even if you did everything you're supposed to do—got your feet right, looked at his belly button, positioned yourself, wrapped him up—he still would run past you. He had great vision and great feet ... If you didn't get his feet, you weren't going to get him."

— Mike Singletary, former NFL Chicago Bears Linebacker

"He was a great runner, because he was so well prepared, but also he had great instincts. He had a vision on the field that few people have—knowing when a hole was opening up, seeing something downfield that nobody else saw. It's like he had a sixth sense."

— Wayne Fontes, former Detroit Lions Head Coach

"You knew on any given play, he could go all the way, and that made you give a little extra."

— Kevin Glover, former Detroit Lions Teammate

About Barry Sanders

Barry Sanders, during his incredible career with the Detroit Lions, won Rookie of the Year, led the league in rushing multiple times, was named to the Pro Bowl nine times, rushed for 2,053 yards in one season, won the MVP award, registered 10 consecutive 1,000 or more yards per season and gained more than 15,200 yards over his career.

Barry begins this book with the heartfelt details of his family growing up in Wichita, Kansas, and also shares his struggles to earn a place on a sports team, to his relationship with the media throughout his professional career. Barry opens up about his career, his love for the game and his decision to retire when he did. From winning the Heisman Trophy, to being named into the Hall of Fame, Barry details every step of his career and after football.

This book is filled with his relationships with family, friends, teammates and coaches. There's also commentary from players and coaches, including Emmitt Smith, Mike Singletary, Lomas Brown, Wayne Fontes, Kevin Glover, Louis Oliver and Dale Burkholder.

Dedication

In loving memory of my sister and Father …
Nancy and "Deddy." We miss you every day.

In memory of Cecil Wilson, my good friend,
taken from us way too soon.

Last, I dedicate this to the fans.
We shared an incredible 10-year ride
that has become a lifetime bond I truly cherish.

Acknowledgments

THANKS TO:

Lauren, B.J., Nigel, Nick, Noah, Mom, Dad and the entire Sanders Family. Mark E. McCormick, J.B. Bernstein, the late John Madden, all my teammates at Wichita North, Oklahoma State University and in Detroit. Coach Dale Burkholder, Coach Pat Jones, Coach Wayne Fontes, Coach Bobby Ross and all the assistant coaches on their staffs. To those who wrote sidebars for the book (Lomas Brown, Emmitt Smith, Mike Singletary, Wayne Fontes, Louis Oliver, Kevin Glover), Adam Torres, Chirag Sagar and Hillary Crawford. Bo Rader and The Wichita Eagle, Amazon Studios, Amazon Originals, NFL Films, the NFL Network, NFL Properties, NFL Player's Inc., NFL Photos, the Ford Family, the Detroit Lions, Oklahoma State University, Wichita North High School, Rod Wood, Emily Griffin, Bill Keenist, Steve Sabol, Ross Ketover, Jessica Boddy, Ken Rodgers, Sean Greene, Tracy Perlman, Dexter Santos, Muneer Moore, Rob Whalen, Mick Thompson, Kayse Shrum, Larry Reece, Steve Buzzard, Tom Dirato, ESPN, CBS, FOX, ABC, The Heisman Trophy Trust, The College Football Hall of Fame, the NCAA Hall of Champions and the Pro Football Hall of Fame.

Photos courtesy of:

Hulton Archive
AP Worldwide
The Wichita Eagle
Oklahoma State University
The Detroit Free Press
Lauren Sanders, with theElevateProjectInc.com
and TheSONshineProject.org
The Sanders Family
J.B. Bernstein/Access Group of Miami

Cover Photo By:

Amazon Content Services LLC

TABLE OF CONTENTS

INTRODUCTION

By John Madden

On the annual Thanksgiving Day game, I used to give a "turkey leg" to the players who had a great game. Barry Sanders was one of those guys who you could give the leg to as soon as the turkey was finished cooking. In every game, he made moves that you'd never seen before, moves that made you say, "This can't be." He was the first guy I remember who could do what is now called a "jump cut," where the player jumps in the air and changes direction. When he started doing that move, we didn't even have a name for it.

During his career, players on other teams would talk about how hard he was to tackle. You didn't just miss a tackle, you got embarrassed. The defenders didn't like seeing themselves later on television or on a highlight reel looking silly. When you asked them about trying to tackle Barry Sanders, a lot of them would mention that.

Every person who was in the game at that time said, "Barry is the guy who I would pay to go see." Of course, that's a cliché used by people who never really pay to see games, but it's a way of saying that a player is special.

As his career developed, we came to appreciate that he was someone truly special. There are good running backs, and then there are some backs who play at a completely different level. Walter Payton was a great running back, because he could do everything—run and catch the ball and block.

Emmitt Smith, in his prime, had everything. Barry was on that level, too.

But he was more than a unique player on the field. He was unique off the field. And everyone who knew him felt that way. I've learned through the years that players can't help being jealous of other players. When you interview them, they'll rarely talk in glowing terms about another player. They'd rather talk about themselves. If they're going to say something nice about another player, they'll talk about a teammate. But I've never heard a single player say something negative about Barry. Guys from other teams would talk about him as if they were talking about a teammate. They mostly would talk about how classy he was.

He was the most unassuming superstar I've ever met. He mentioned to me once that he was taking college classes at Oakland University in the suburbs of Detroit, during the season. He's a famous athlete, a local hero and he's taking classes! I said, "How can you do that?" He said, "They don't know I'm there." I said, "How can they not know?" He said, "Because I don't tell them."

> One of the things I enjoyed about Barry Sanders was the way he'd nonchalantly handed the ball to the official after a touchdown—as if it were no big deal.

Most guys want to be noticed after a touchdown. They're doing their celebrations, dancing around or jumping into the stands. Barry became the exception. He got more notice for not celebrating. When he scored or did something amazing, that was sufficient. He didn't need to do anything else.

He was always very approachable—so cooperative, in fact, that it was tempting to take him for granted and ask him anything. I was talking to him one time about his new contract, and I said, "How much do you make?" He looked at me, and said, "How much do you make?" I thought, okay, that's right. It's none of my business. But he was so unassuming you'd forget that.

I got to know him well during his career, and I also heard about him from other players who had Barry Sanders stories. Lomas Brown, for example, started a second career telling Barry Sanders stories. And every married guy who played for the Lions had stories about Barry coming by for dinner and about how much he could eat. He was a little guy, but I guess he ate a lot. Then after dinner he'd lay on the floor with the kids and play with

Barry Sanders is shown eating a turkey leg.

them, get them all worked up, and then he'd leave while the kids were still bouncing off the walls. The guys who played with him, his teammates, loved him.

To understand the true Barry Sanders, remember the way he left football. That was pure Barry. He played his last game without telling anyone. There were no parades, no big "Barry Sanders Day," nothing like that. When he was finished he walked away. Everyone was upset with him, because he did it his way; he didn't do it their way.

At the time, some people thought his retirement was a ploy to get a better contract. But knowing Barry, I knew it wasn't a ploy. He doesn't do things that way. At the same time, even though I had gotten to know him, I had no indication that he was planning to retire. I didn't see it coming. Some guys will talk about retiring before they do it. They'll let you know they're thinking about it, but not Barry. He wasn't a big talker. When he was finished, he was finished. It was frustrating for him, I think, to be such a great player and play for a team that didn't win. A player like that wants to win a Super Bowl.

When you lose a superstar like Barry Sanders, it takes something out of the game for a while. His absence was particularly noticeable on Thanksgiving Day. Detroit was never all that good, but they had the tradition of playing on the holiday, and you could always count on Barry Sanders doing something miraculous. He became part of the tradition. On Thanksgiving Day, you knew you were going to get to see Barry Sanders play.

I picked him for a lot of the annual All-Madden teams, because he was my kind of player. If somebody asks what you want in a running back, you have to answer, "I want Barry Sanders." He was the whole package. You wouldn't take him, only because he could break away for a touchdown on any play, even though he could do that. You would take him, because he had all the ingredients. He was the guy you wanted on your side.

He could do anything. And he got along with everyone. His teammates love d him. When kids in his neighborhood were choosing sides for a game, he was probably always picked first. He was probably never it in tag.

Barry was truly special in a lot of ways, and anybody who is a real football fan misses seeing Barry Sanders play.

CHAPTER ONE

Volutsia's Calling

I was born and raised in Wichita, Kansas, a city with a rich and interesting history, most of which I've learned from my friend, Mark, who has a keen interest in the subject. A local historian tells the story how, in 1750, a group of French explorers, in search of gold, unwittingly founded the city. As the explorers navigated the Arkansas River (and that's pronounced R-Kansas) to its source at the foot of the Rocky Mountains, they came across a Spanish pack train loaded with gold. The French robbed the Spanish, filled the boats with gold and headed back down the river.

Barry Sanders is shown in his elementary school photo.

When they approached an island where the Arkansas and Little Arkansas rivers meet, they made camp.

That night, they were attacked by Native Americans, and only one man escaped to tell the story. He never came back for the gold, but a later map showed the area now known as Wichita, marked as a gold mine. And as people arrived in search of gold, Wichita was born.

Legendary lawman Bat Masterson called the area home. Wyatt Earp was fired by the City of Wichita after prostitution money he collected went missing. Billy the Kid witnessed numerous gunfights in the city, and his mother's signature is on the city's charter. By June of 1887, the city ranked third nationally in volume of real estate transactions behind only New York and Kansas City, and ahead of Chicago and Philadelphia. Town leaders nicknamed Wichita "The Peerless Princess of the Prairie." Shortly after, an economic crisis crippled the town and rolled back the rapid expansion. People left almost as quickly as they'd come.

Grit and enterprise, however, saved the town. Walt Anderson, who founded White Castle hamburgers in the city, helped to usher in a tradition of entrepreneurship. The country's first Phillips 66 gas station opened in Wichita. Walter Beech and Clyde Cessna built an aircraft industry that marked the city as the "Air Capital of the World." Frank and Dan Carney borrowed $600 from their mother to found what would become the international restaurant icon Pizza Hut. Perhaps, as the historian says in her article, there may actually have been gold here.

I was born here—on July 16, 1968. My childhood wasn't much different from the average American childhood. I had an older brother, who used to hold me down and punch the air out of my chest. We threw rocks at each other, played basketball and tackle-the-man-with-the-ball all day. We rode our bicycles in the summer, swam at McAdams Park pool and ate penny candy until our bellies swelled.

Barry Sanders, is shown in the front row, third from the right, is shown in elementary school, with his football team. His brother, Byron, is in the middle of the second row, number 44.

The two-block stretch of North Volutsia I grew up on, however, was special. It could have set the gold standard for achievement most anywhere in White or Black America.

Between my house at 2049 and the house at 1922, Black parents raised a doctor who practiced in Kansas City, a federal agent for the Internal Revenue Service, an airplane pilot, an Ebony fashion model, a preacher, a host of teachers and college graduates with advanced degrees, two journalists, at least three nurses and one All-Pro running back.

These children were raised by parents who were teachers, pilots, a state representative, a construction company owner, nurses and blue-collar laborers. They were all special people drawn to a special place.

KANSAS AND WICHITA IN BLACK HISTORY

As I turned pro, I often was asked by Black people who learned I was from Wichita, "Are there Blacks in Kansas?" I assured them there were many Blacks. I was an adult before I realized

Barry Sanders, is shown seated far left in elementary school, with his Biddy Basketball team.

the pivotal role Kansas played in Black history. Again, my friend, Mark, told me a good many of these facts. Kansas entered the Union in 1861 as a free state, and its first years were troubled by violence, as the national issue of slavery boiled into the start of the Civil War. Statehood did not come to Kansas without a significant cost in human life. Abolitionist John Brown led numerous raids and battles to maintain that status and helped earn the state the name "Bleeding Kansas."

The state has produced many distinguished Black Americans. Filmmaker, author and Pulitzer-prize winning photographer Gordon Parks was from Ft. Scott, Kansas. Langston Hughes, the poet laureate of Harlem, called Kansas home in his childhood, as did Gwendolyn Brooks, the first Black woman to win a Pulitzer Prize in literature.

And so when I'm asked if there are Black people in Kansas, the answer is "Yep," and none of the Black folks anywhere in the country could have had any semblance of freedom, if not for our people's history in my home state. When the U.S. Supreme Court took up the issue of school desegregation in 1954, in the now famous case of Brown v. Board of Education of Topeka,

Barry Sanders is shown in elementary school, with his football team.

Kansas, the people of Topeka found themselves at the center of what would be a landmark decision to begin breaking down decades-old racial boundaries.

Many Wichitans believe the nation's first successful, student-led lunch counter sit-in took place in downtown Wichita, in 1958. Members of an NAACP youth group started the protest at Dockum's drug store downtown. Led by a young man named Ronald Walters, the students' campaign successfully opened the store's lunch counter to Black citizens, who previously had to place orders at the back door and eat in the alley.

Walters would grow up to become one of the nation's foremost political scientists and intellectuals. He served as the Rev. Jesse Jackson's campaign manager in Jackson's 1984 bid for the presidency, directed the floor operations during the 1988 Democratic National Convention and offered political commentary on a variety of network cable news programs, such as CNN's Crossfire. Walters grew up on Madison, just a few blocks away from my childhood home on North Volutsia.

I spent hours shooting hoops and playing bumper pool in the recreation center designed by Black Wichita Blue-blood Charles McAfee. McAfee's family arrived with the city's earliest settlers,

Barry Sanders is shown in high school, with his basketball team.

and his architectural works earned him a chapter in the book *Black Genius*. Though his buildings in Wichita and across the country have won numerous architectural awards, he's perhaps best known for the work done by the Atlanta arm of his firm, run by his daughter, Cheryl, in designing all 32 Olympic venues for the 1996 Olympics in Atlanta.

McAfee grew up several blocks away from my childhood home, in an area that served as the business and cultural center of town for Black citizens in segregated Wichita.

During his childhood, that neighborhood produced a dozen African-Americans with doctoral degrees, virtually all of whom had to leave the city in search of career opportunities elsewhere. One Wichitan who left was Donald Hollowell, who may be the best known in civil rights circles as the lawyer who helped free the Rev. Martin Luther King, Jr., from the brutal confines of Reidsville Prison in Georgia, where he was confined for a creative traffic violation charge. But he's also the man who gave Washington, D.C., Powerbroker Vernon Jordan his first job and was the courageous lawyer who defended Black clients in front of all-white juries in dangerous rural areas—and won.

The stubborn focus on education and achievement that drove these people, surely influenced my parents' generation, who worked hard to make sure the elevator to success didn't leave without their children.

SPORTS

It would be difficult to underestimate the importance of sports in my childhood. Daddy, a lifelong fan of the Kansas Jayhawk basketball team and Oklahoma Sooner football team, always seemed to have the chatter of the game on the television or on the radio. And in the barbershop, we'd listen to the heated arguments among the old men about the failings and fortunes of local and regional teams.

From the time my brother, Byron, and I were small, Daddy enrolled us in Biddy Basketball and Little League football. We had electric football sets and Oakland Raiders winter coats and ski caps. Our lives as children revolved around sports. At school, after school and on Saturdays, we'd gather in corner lots and sometimes crawl over the fence at Wichita State University's football stadium, or line the walls of the basement in what is now Lynette Woodard Recreation Center. We'd play pick-up basketball games at the center until Cliff Fanning, who ran the place, chased us off the court.

If we couldn't play basketball at the center, we'd rip the spokes out of a bicycle wheel and nail the rim to a tree for a hoop. For pick-up football games, we'd mark off a field on a duplex lawn and designate a tree as one end zone and a sidewalk as the other. On Friday nights in the fall, we'd pile into the back of Daddy's pick-up and watch high school football games and play tackle-the-man on the sidelines at halftime.

We regarded the older athletes around us—neighborhood starts from the court, track or football field—with awe. We felt this way toward these guys, because of the city's and the state's rich sports tradition.

Local lore says the basketball fast break was created at Wichita East High School by legendary head coach Ralph Miller, who later coached at the University of Iowa. East High also produced legendary miler Jim Ryun.

In 1988, the year I won the Heisman Trophy, the University of Kansas, led by forward Danny Manning and Coach Larry Brown, won the NCAA championship. The next year, Wichita State University won the College World Series. Sports seemed to bring us together in a way nothing else could.

In our neighborhood, we were generally safe among the blocks and blocks of modest, lower middle-class homes. Most families had children, and we all played football and basketball together in the parks and lots dotting what was then called Northeast Wichita. But the streets did call out to a lot of people, and more than a few answered. We had friends lured by the siren call of life on street corners.

The older we got, the wider the concentric circles of our lives began taking in people who lived on delinquency's edge. Most of us stayed out of trouble and laughed at friends who smoked weed and drank Canadian Mist. But as graduation approached and life paths beyond North High grew clouded, more and more of us made the leap from the curb into the street.

But Volutsia had another sort of calling, too.

The adults who raised us called on us to work hard and to stretch that work into some sort of future for ourselves. We also chose diverse career paths, as I said before. The differences in those paths indicates to me that we didn't simply select jobs or even careers. We followed a calling, a choice of life's work we not only enjoyed, but also helped to define us. That we aimed so high and dreamed so creatively, spoke well of the spirit our parents had cultivated in us. They fought the "clouds of inferiority," which the Rev. Martin Luther King, Jr., had said formed in the minds of Black children.

We could do whatever we wanted and go wherever we wanted, just as long as we made the right choices. My parents, my neighborhood, and the great history and traditions of Wichita helped me make those choices.

WORDS FROM MARK MCCORMICK LIFELONG FRIEND

A person could backstroke in all of the Barry Sanders lore, floating out there in the pop culture sea. Can you separate the fact from the fiction in the following tales?

- *He once swallowed a straight pin he used as a toothpick, and had to sit out a game his sophomore year in high school.*
- *During two-a-day practices in high school, he attended the first practice, spent the day roofing with his father in hundred-degree heat, and then returned for the evening practice.*
- *For a brief period, he averaged 30 yards per carry in high school.*
- *He can throw a football with either hand.*
- *When he was younger, he could dunk a basketball from a flat-footed stance under the basket.*
- *He could eat a loaf of bread in one sitting.*
- *He had a dog that ran the length of the football field during a halftime show at a Wichita State University home game.*
- *He once played electric football for 16 straight hours.*
- *He frequently found himself standing in the corner of Ms. Boyd's third-grade classroom, holding a stack of dictionaries, and standing on one leg.*
- *He'd obnoxiously honk like a goose in class behind the teacher's back.*

Barry Sanders in elementary school, is shown with his lifelong friend, Mark McCormick. This photo was taken by Sharon Wasson.

It can be difficult to separate the real from the surreal with Barry, but I know the man. The Barry I know stayed up late into the night to help me piece together the bicycle I needed to get to and from summer football workouts in high school. He knew how much I wanted to play. He's the person who, before sports fans swooned at the mention of his name, offered to split his grant money with me when he learned I was struggling to stay in college.

He's the intellectually curious man who, as he's reading a book, copies definitions of words he doesn't know in an accompanying notebook for future reference. He's the generous friend, who has exposed me to so much (from the Cannes Film Festival in France to Copacabana Beach in Rio de Janeiro) and opened so many opportunities (such as helping him write this book) that I couldn't begin to repay him.

He's the philanthropist, who cares about people's struggles and relishes the prospect of helping people, and then retreating, so as not to draw attention to himself. He's the friend who'd rather march in your parade than lead his own. The Barry I know loves to laugh.

The truth is—all these stories are true. It has been amazing to see him move from the rough-housing boy I knew back on Volutsia, to the savvy businessman and doting father he is today. In Barry's case at least, all the lore and urban myth in the world can't hold a candle to the truth about him as a person.

CHAPTER TWO

Mother

I would not have been as successful in football without the help of my mother, Shirley Sanders. I don't think she knows much about how to break down defenses, and she never once instructed me on the mechanics of taking a hand-off or making defenders miss, but she may have been my finest coach.

Barry Sanders and his mother, Shirley Sanders, at Georgio's Restaurant in Wichita, Kan., following the NFL Draft.

I've never seen her emotionally shaken. I have never seen her lose it. I have never seen her discouraged to the point where she wanted to give up. She was a strong and resilient person with great emotional balance. As a player, I could sense her composure in my approach to the game. Through her, I learned to develop the resilience and balance I used on the field. A friend of mine told me that Tiger Woods' mother—and her Buddhist influence—might hold the key to Tiger's success. Tiger's ability to summon a deep calm under pressure separates him from his peers. The same is true for my mother. She gave me the ability to stay calm under pressure.

Many times in my playing career, if not most of the time, I faced defenses designed to stop my team's running game. The other team had 11 players on the field focused mostly on playing the run, and targeting me. On a lot of plays, they had some success shutting me down. They'd manage to wall me in, swarm me, hold me to a yard or two, or even stop me behind the line of scrimmage. And they wouldn't simply try to stop me; they'd try to demoralize me. Discourage me.

Late in the game, my stat sheet would read something like: 1 yard, 2 yards, 0 yards. But I'd keep coming, play after play, quarter after quarter. Then, somehow, I'd find a way to exploit some small error—a missed tackle, a poor pursuit angle—and 60 yards later, I was handing the ball to the ref. Mother raised us that way: to be faithful; to keep pushing; to not give up; and to smile along the way. Those qualities served me well on the field and in life.

Her tenacity was just one of the gifts she gave to me. She is also the genealogical benefactor I should thank for my heavily muscled legs, my most valuable asset as a player.

I got my build from her side of the family, the Fishers. I've always been told, especially by my sister, Nancy, that I have "Fisher legs," meaning muscled quads and calves.

My maternal grandfather, Johnny Fisher, also had big calves. Grandpa Fisher was a brick mason, who inspired awe and respect in my father, by once going to work on a broken leg. He just propped up his leg and continued laying bricks. I can see him in my mother. She has an incredible gift for tenderness, but she also has toughness. She ran our home that way.

Throughout my childhood, we had a decent meal everyday, but I never remember her sitting down to eat. She was always taking care of us. In fact, she rarely got to have anything for herself. She used to like to drink Dr. Pepper, and sometimes she'd go off somewhere in the house to try to enjoy one. All of us kids would be in the den, but when we heard that top pop, we'd all converge on her for a sip.

It never seemed to bother her. She had a way of endlessly giving, without appearing as if we were taking from her, or that

Barry Sanders is shown with his mother, Shirley Sanders, sitting on the sideline at the Pro Bowl. He says he always feels good when he is with his mom.

our requests taxed her at all. Mother cares about everyone who comes in contact with her. She cares about what they're going through and what they're facing on any given day. A lot of people can act like they care about the concerns of other people, but she really does care.

All of her strength comes from her faith in God. When I was young, she'd get up every morning and pray, and on many nights, we'd have a big family prayer. We all would sit in a circle and each of us, in turn, would say a brief prayer, and then we'd finish with "The Lord's Prayer." Her faith was the source of what we saw as an endless supply of patience and kindness.

But she was no pushover.

As the case with most teenagers, I often wanted to hang out with my friends on Friday night. One time, I asked her if I could go out with them, having done it the previous week.

She said, "No, you're not going to do that."

The same thing happened when I asked her if I could get a BB gun. Everyone had one, and I wanted one, too.

"No," she said. "We're not having any guns in this house."

After she said "no" in a certain way, I knew there was no more negotiating about it. She said it the way it needed to be said. Sometimes, you knew you could explore why she felt that way, and sometimes, you knew not to say anything more. When it came to things like sleepovers at a friend's house, she was actually quicker to say "no" than my father. She wanted to know where we were and who we were with so she wouldn't have to worry about us.

And if there was any worrying to do, she wanted to do it. She still makes us feel safer when we're with her, but that feeling was especially strong when we were kids.

She was the shelter. I'm sure it was difficult running that household and taking care of all of us, but she wanted that burden on her own shoulders. She wanted to make sure that whatever was happening, it became her struggle, not our own struggle.

I remember picking up the phone once when I was a child, and the guy on the other end said that if he didn't receive the overdue house payment, something bad was going to happen. But I don't recall ever feeling we were in danger of being kicked out. My mother wanted to protect us from such things, and she didn't let us know when she was worried about those things. I think she loved her role as mother and protector.

She grew up in a similar family. She was raised in Wagoner, Oklahoma, which is little more than a cluster of tiny homes clinging to the rolling prairie near Tulsa.

She was the oldest of 11 children, and so she was almost a second mother in that home, inheriting a number of maternal duties, in addition to her own set of chores. Winter on the plains can be particularly harsh. Lashing winds slice their way over the flat landscape, and Mother spent many such days having to leave school in those winds to feed the family's hogs.

She met Daddy, when they were students at Horace Mann Junior High School, after her family moved to Wichita. At 19, she married the sweet, industrious little boy, who always had a job, and who always had money enough to offer her candy. They eventually had 11 children of her own. I was the seventh.

She raised us, took us to church, cooked, cleaned and somehow had the focus and the drive to return to school and earn a nursing certificate from Wichita State University.

Through the years, our relationship has matured seamlessly. There was never a time when we suffered an abrupt change between us. Only now, as I look back from the perspective of being an adult and a parent, can I see the subtle changes that did take place. As I grew up, she saw that I was changing from a boy into a man, and she treated me accordingly.

When I was at Oklahoma State trying to decide if I should enter the NFL draft, she advised me, giving me her opinion on what I should do. But she let me make the final decision on my own. Some parents are always going to see you as their child and feel they have a right to tell you what to do. They have a hard time living with the fact that their kids are now grown.

But Mother is so insightful that she seemed to have been thinking about our own relationship changing long before the changes occurred. There weren't any bumps. I always knew I could tell her anything, and I knew that when I did tell her something, the information was as safe as it could get. She wouldn't tell anyone.

I remember having to tell her that B.J., my first son, was on the way. I felt strange telling her the news, because I was not married to B.J.'s mother. I knew I had to tell her about B.J., as well as about the decision not to get married. She was surprised, and I'm sure she was a little hurt, though she didn't express those feelings. She took the news in her usual calm way.

I see her influence in my everyday life, and she has shaped the way I view the world: Try to be considerate of other people and put everything into your kids. It must work for her. I've rarely seen her discouraged or unhappy.

CHAPTER THREE

I'm Not Your Friend, I'm Your Father

My daddy sat in his easy chair, a University of Kansas basketball game flickering on the television in front of him. My son, Nigel, four months old at the time, sat in his lap, staring in the direction of the screen, as if he could follow the Xs and Os of the game. Daddy's calloused palms tenderly covered the baby's tummy and chest. Now and then, Nigel would squirm or squawk, and Daddy would offer a firm, but gentle, "Hey, all right now."

Barry Sanders is shown with his father, William Sanders, at the Pro Bowl.

As we chatted on that January evening about the Jayhawk's chances for the season, it occurred to me that until the previous November, just two months before, we hadn't talked for an entire year. Until a confrontation occurred in the kitchen, just a room away from where we were sitting, he'd been the nuts and bolts of every part of my life. But in that year, I'd settled into retirement, gotten engaged, gotten married, started a new career in business and brought home my second son without him.

Yet here we sat, talking sports, while he held my son. Who'd have thought that someone only 21-inches long could bridge all the miles of misunderstanding between my father and me? We obviously love each other, but in the preceding years and months, we collided like rams.

I sometimes wondered if I was ever quite the son he thought I should be. His way of raising us never made sense to me, until I was older.

Daddy once said that most little boys have no fear when with their father. "A father could jump in a gasoline ocean with a torch in his ass, and most little boys would jump in after him," he said. "But not Barry. Barry was always different."

I've been close to my mother for as far back as I can remember. I can recall clinging to her apron in our kitchen, following her from the fridge to the sink to the stove. When Daddy saw this, he growled that a boy shouldn't follow his mother around like that. Pretty soon, he said, I was going to be out working with him, where I belonged.

He terrified me at times. I've always maintained a healthy fear of him, starting with the day one of the kids in the house stole some quarters he'd kept in a shoe in his closet. When no one confessed, he lined all of us up and whipped us. I was five. My emotions toward him baffled me. I feared him and I loved him, all at the same time.

Many nights at the dinner table, I'd fume. My mother, my brother, my sisters and I would all be sitting around the table, knives and forks in hand, a dish of sweet, steamy food placed in the middle of the table—waiting. No one could eat until Daddy (a name we pronounced "Deddy") came home and sat down. And when he did, no one could speak. I never understood that.

He never understood me either. Daddy, from time to time, slept outside, because he loved the outdoors. He'd sleep in our screened-in porch, or on one of the picnic tables he'd hammered together in the backyard, or right on the lush green lawn he clipped and edged with mathematical precision. He once asked me to sleep out there with him, and I said, "No." I must have been seven or eight then. He couldn't believe it. It hurt him. But as much as that may have hurt him, it was a footrace that never happened that wounded him much more deeply.

Mother said Daddy talked about it for years. Daddy was a fantastic athlete in his own right. He once was offered a tryout with the Oakland Raiders, but his growing family—I think he had three children at the time—prevented him from following through. That's likely why he was always so harsh in his attitude toward girls and us having girlfriends, but that's another story. Daddy was a very fast runner. He could outrun us for short distances—him running backwards and us running forwards—until we got to high school. But a friend of mine, Derrick Parker, beat Daddy one day. And Derrick didn't just beat Daddy; he strutted around and teased him afterward.

Daddy was furious. It got so bad that Daddy made my brother, Byron, race Derrick, but Derrick beat Byron, too. I was a couple of blocks away, shooting baskets at an outdoor court, when one of my cousins ran up and told me that Daddy wanted me to come home and race Derrick. I said, "No."

I felt really uncomfortable. Daddy didn't wear embarrassment well. The whole incident hurt his pride. But I just couldn't see going back and racing Derrick for that. I have competitive fire, but this just seemed ridiculous. He later said that if anyone had beaten his father and then strutted around afterwards, he'd make the guy race him until he'd saved face for his father. Or, he'd fight the guy. He said he loved his father that much. I can only imagine what he must have thought of me when I decided not to race.

That was the first time I had refused a specific order from him. But over the next few years, the air between us would crackle from the tension. One of the worst moments came shortly before the NFL draft deadline, when Daddy cornered me and cussed me out for even considering staying at Oklahoma State for my senior year. I'd never seen him that way, so emotional. He was right in my face, screaming. He was almost in tears. I relented, obviously, and entered the draft.

Through the money I made in my career, I was able to do things for him that I'd always wanted to do. He'd spent years

William Sanders is shown with his daughters, from left, Krista, Elissa and Gina.

climbing up and down ladders, carrying circular saws and enormous flaps of shingles on a back that 40 pounds of pressure should have snapped. With the money I was able to give him, he didn't have to do anything. He had no bills, a sprawling home on a man-made pond and several vehicles. He could travel when and where he liked. But whatever I gave him never seemed to be enough. When I decided to set a limit, he exploded.

In the kitchen, in the home I'd bought for him in Wichita, he was bitterly explaining to me what I should be doing with my money. Much of that "advice" had to do with giving him more of it. Our relationship was at stake, he said, and before leaving the room, he approached me menacingly. That was the last time we would speak for a year.

Two weeks before my wedding, I invited him to Las Vegas for a fundraiser. I wanted to talk to him. I needed his advice. I needed him to be there with me. But he decided not to come, and then conspicuously skipped my wedding. Looking back, I can see that the whole episode was a function of the changes within our relationship.

I remember one day, for example, when I was walking with him and a young man I'd hired to care for the lawn at his house. We were walking the property line, and Daddy was pointing here and there, explaining how he wanted things done. Before long, talking almost exclusively to the young man, he launched into a painful story about his past.

He said when he was young, he had dreamed of being a printer. He read books about it and prepared himself for a career by picking up odd jobs. He eventually landed a job as a printer, but being the industrious teenager he was, he also worked as a janitor at the Air Force base. When he arrived late to deliver plans for a printing job, he found a "closed" sign in the window, and went on to his next job.

He found out later that despite the sign, the customer had still been waiting for him inside. Daddy was fired the next day. He said he thanked God that every time he lost a job, he got a better one, but he told the story in a way that made it clear he still felt cheated. I had never heard that story, and I wondered why he was willing to open himself so earnestly to a stranger, and yet, he had never shared the story with a son who loved him. Then I thought of something he told Byron and me once: "I'm not your friend, I'm your father."

One of my father's faults was that he was unable to see our conflicts for what they were: healthy. As painful as it was, it was healthy. It was the way it should have been. Separation. That's the word. At some point, a child must separate from the parent and begin to live his own life and make his own decisions. We don't always choose when that time comes. Sometimes, it can be harder for the parent than for the child. I think I now can understand why it was so difficult for him.

His life was difficult. He was preparing his children for the 1937 world he was born into as a Black man. It was a tough world. It was mean. It was unfair. And, at times, he was all of those things to us. But what I now understand is that he was making sure we would face nothing out in the world that he hadn't prepared us for. People think they knew him, but they didn't.

They have no idea how significant he was. They saw the proud father grabbing the microphone, filling the reporter's notebooks and soaking up the glow of his son's celebrity. But those sound bites lie about his significance.

Daddy made the world work. He took care of his family, worshiped God and contributed to his community as a good neighbor. He loved people, he loved to laugh and his friends said he was one heck of a friend.

You couldn't know him, unless you were around him. Unfortunately, people only got to know him in those lying sound bites. They didn't know how significant he was, but I hope he knew how important he was to me and to the family. He laid the groundwork for who I am. He's been a part of every part of my life. He was the difference between me and the many talented athletes who had shimmering futures in the palms of their hands and squandered them in bottles of alcohol and pinches of white powder.

Coming to my Little League games, coming to school, taking me to work with him—those things will follow me from now on, and will help shape the lives of my children. It is hard to express his significance to me, but I was reminded of it with the feelings I had when I was able to watch him with Nigel.

CHAPTER FOUR

Stature of Limitations

I guess everyone hides a bit of insecurity. I'm not talking about the whiny, wimpy form of insecurity, but instead a healthy concern about one's own limits, an awareness of the boundaries and the outermost confines of abilities. Without those concerns, without that focus and attention, how can you ever push beyond them? How do you keep from resting on what you've already accomplished?

Barry Sanders is shown in his high school Redskins football uniform.

My challenge has always been my stature. From the time I played Little League ball, coaches didn't think I measured up. Some played me, others benched me, but virtually everyone doubted me. And that's saying something in Little League, where the players usually weigh only 50 or 60 pounds. But I was small, even for my age. I often held the title of smallest on the team.

In early elementary school, when everyone was roughly the same size, I played quite a bit, and I played well. Though I was small, I was also faster than most everyone and showed it on the field in a number of long touchdown runs.

But when everyone continued to grow, except me, it got more and more difficult to get any playing time. One coach wouldn't play me, because I had a heart murmur—a gurgling sound in my heart caused by irregularly closing heart valves. Most murmurs are not dangerous, but they can be caused by blood flowing through a damaged or overworked heart, and valve disease may result.

When Daddy found out the reason I wasn't playing, he was angry. He pulled me out of school to go to the hospital for a battery of tests that turned up nothing. Doctors gave me the go-ahead. But the coach wouldn't budge. Despite the fact that I was good enough to play, I sat the bench a lot. He just thought I was too small and wanted to start someone else, a fantastic player in his own right—a guy named Kenneth "Dabby" Dawson, who went on to play at the University of Wyoming. I would play against him in the 1988 Holiday Bowl.

Don't get me wrong. There were good players on the team who deserved to start, but I deserved some playing time, too. Maybe it was my size, or maybe it was the heart murmur. To this day, I don't know.

WICHITA NORTH

High school wasn't a lot different. I attended Wichita North and was proud to represent my school. Both of my parents went there. I started at tailback on the sophomore team, but in my junior year, my brother, Byron, started at tailback and was outstanding. That year, the varsity coach, Bob Shepler, recognized my speed and started me at defensive back. I also returned punts and kickoffs. By returning punts, kicks and interceptions to the end zone, I led the team in touchdowns that year.

Because of that success, in my senior year I expected to start at tailback. Byron had graduated, and I had proven I could run. Instead, I started as a wingback, basically a wide receiver, while a talented underclassman named Orlando Parker got the tailback position. Coach Shepler had moved on to become the athletic director, and we had a new coach, Dale Burkholder, but I found out later that Parker was Shepler's choice. Shepler thought I was too small for the position and told the new coach not to put me at tailback. He also had another complaint about me—he thought I lacked "contact courage," meaning I was afraid of being hit, afraid to run directly into the line or into a defender. Two other coaches on the staff said Shepler mentioned to them that I had a yellow streak up my back.

Barry Sanders is shown in his homecoming king crown for his high school.

He apparently came to that conclusion based on my running style. Shepler wanted backs to run to an assigned spot, whether a hole had opened there or not, but I'd get the ball and move like a tremor wherever I could find cracks in the defense. To be fair, the coaching staff probably hadn't seen anyone with my combination of short stature and frenetic running style. There weren't a lot of role models.

However, Coach Burkholder, who we called Coach B, recognized my unique abilities and eventually would move me in as the starting tailback. Coach B was new-school and Shepler was old-school. Coach B cracked jokes and made his sometimes difficult practices fun. He was all enthusiasm. Before practice, and sometimes during drills, he would chant, "It's great to be young, alive and a Redskin." I realize that my high school retired that mascot and adopted a new one, "Red Hawks," and I respect that decision. But we had the love for that school drilled into us.

Before the first game, Coach B closed us up in a gymnasium until it was time to board the team bus. He wanted us to meditate, concentrate, envision what we were about to do. We all spread out on the floor of the darkened gym. Some people relaxed quietly, others mumbled to themselves, some fell asleep.

Not me.

I couldn't sit still. The insecurity bug nibbled at me. My heart thumped under my pads. I got up. I sat down again. I just wanted to get it over with—to get on the bus, get to the field and start the game. One of the reasons I stopped running track as a kid, was because I hated those endless, tension-filled times before the race.

The pressure was simply overwhelming. But whatever doubts I felt that night were unfounded. I scored on four dramatic runs, racking up 157 yards off gadget plays from my wingback position. That's 30 yards per carry. After the game, I'm certain Coach B wanted to move me back to tailback, but he was meeting resistance from Shepler. It was the size thing again, as well as his concerns about my "contact courage."

Coach B finally pulled the trigger, going into our fourth game of the season, which was against South High. I think that game offered the first glimpse into the kind of running back I would become. I rang up 274 yards and four touchdowns, not including a 50-yard reception, which was called back because of a penalty.

The play started with a simple toss to the right, but that run had more stops and changes of direction than an airport flight line. I took the toss and drifted to the right, drawing in the defense, veering away from a lineman, who already crossed the line of scrimmage. When I reached the corner, the tight end was still on his man to my outside shoulder, but four other defenders closed in from the left.

Sensing they were approaching too quickly, I stopped abruptly, cut left and watched them tumble into each other. I swiveled out of the cut and turned up field, but having come to a complete stop, I'd given a linebacker time to almost catch me. I stopped again and then jumped. His momentum carried him past me, his arm on my waist, his cleats airborne. Changing direction in the air, I darted forward.

The first set of defenders who had run past me, now had recovered, and they were rushing toward me. I bolted up field with a fast defender out ahead of me and to my right, bearing down on the area between the hash marks and attempting to cut off my path to the end zone. I put on a burst and flashed past him before he could cut me off, and then flicked off the last defender with a stutter-step and trotted into the end zone. After the game, Coach B told reporters that the play showed my natural acumen for running the ball.

"It was one of the greatest runs I've ever seen by a high school running back," he said. "I said, 'My Lord.' Not many people could ever do this. If they just went out in their front lawn and tried to do these moves, they'd probably hurt themselves." As he watched the videotape of the run, he said to a reporter, "Look at him reading his blocks, changing his speed. That's natural, God-given talent." His praise meant a lot to me, partly because he had coached Mike Rozier at a Kansas junior college. And he was right about owing my talent to God.

Barry Sanders is shown during a high school basketball game.

On the strength of such performances, I suddenly found myself in the thick of the race for the city league rushing title. You might think I won that race, but I didn't. During our last regular-season game, Coach B told me I was close to the title. The leader in the rushing race was a blue-collar back named Brad Wiesen, who played for one of the two powerhouse Catholic schools in town. He had carried the ball 39 times that night in his bid for the title. Nevertheless, the title fluttered within reach.

I asked Coach B if he thought that we'd put away East High, the team we were playing, and he said, "Yeah." In that game, I already had gained 262 yards, including a 92-yard touchdown, so I told him to leave me on the bench and let some of the other guys play. I cheered them on from the sidelines. Wiesen finished with 1,450 yards on 226 carries for a 6.4 yards-per-carry average. Despite not starting at tailback until the fourth game of the year, I finished with 1,417 yards on 139 carries, a 10.2 yards-per-carry average.

Had I won the rushing title before that point in the game, I would have been fine. I would have liked to win it. But to try to get it after the game was in hand seemed to me to lack dignity. I would do the same thing again as a rookie with the Detroit Lions.

I was about 11 yards from the rushing title when I told the coach, Wayne Fontes,who wanted to put me back in so I could win the title, that I was fine on the bench. It wasn't that I was trying to be modest. It just didn't feel right to focus on an individual award, rather than on what the team needed.

I finished the season with All-City and All-State honors, and even made Honorable Mention All-American. I was named the Most Valuable Player of the annual Shrine Bowl, a charity game showcasing the states' best prep players. You would think with a season like that, the questions and the doubts about me would ease.

Instead, they grew.

Barry Sanders (no. 22) joining in on a tackle during a junior varsity football game his sophomore year at North High School.

WORDS FROM COACH BURKHOLDER FORMER HEAD COACH, WICHITA NORTH

It was the last game of our senior season, and we were winning the ball game. I pulled a lot of the starters, but Barry was in a battle for the city rushing title. In the fourth quarter, we were on the sidelines, and I called him over to ask if he wanted me to put him back in the game so he could get enough yards to win the title. I said, "I can either put you back in, or let the young kids play." In the blink of an eye, he said, "Let the young kids play, Coach." That's Barry.

I wish every coach had the experience of working with a talent and with a kid like Barry Sanders. He was special, a person with a lot of character. He was a quiet kid, never said much, and never gave an excuse. I remember he missed the first practice, and I had to discipline him. He told me he had to finish a construction job with his dad and that he was sorry and wouldn't miss again. One thing about Barry Sanders—you can believe him. He's very true to his word. And he was always willing to play hurt. It bothered me when I would hear, after he made it to the pros, that he wouldn't play hurt. I know different. He would play hurt all the time. He'd lay out for passes that other players would just let go.

He was a team kind of guy. He liked being on a mission with a group of guys. When the team ran onto the field, you were going to see Barry in the middle of a big group. He wasn't going to be the first guy through the bust-away.

He was a very easy player to coach. He was a stickler for the fine points, and he loved being shown. He loved being coached. He was always eager to improve his game. I remember watching him as a pro and saw he was still working to improve, even in his final year. When he was in high school and college, he wasn't a blocker, not that you want a runner like that to do a lot of blocking. But as a pro, he steadily improved that part of his game. He'd put his head right into a rushing linebacker.

In fact, because he was such a stickler, I could tell in his last year or so that he was losing enthusiasm for the game. When he took a hand-off, he was just reaching for the ball with both his hands down. He wasn't keeping his elbows high. That showed me that he'd lost some of his focus.

At North, I imitated the University of Nebraska offense—a Nebraska slot I. We started the season with Barry at the wingback, but in the first game, he scored four times on the wingback reverse. I already had a good player at the I, but Barry was just too good to not put there. No one could tackle him. He wasn't a traditional runner. He ran scared, but that's a pretty damn good way to run. When Barry got the ball, he made things happen.

CHAPTER FIVE

Cowboy Up

Despite a great senior season in 1985, at Wichita North, almost no one recruited me, and certainly not my beloved University of Oklahoma Sooners. Emporia State, Iowa State, Tulsa and eventually Oklahoma State came calling, but I heard nothing from either of the big schools in the state—the University of Kansas and Kansas State University, both of which had programs so bad that they couldn't even beat each other. During one of their games, in the late 1980s, they played to a tie, sending the home-field Jayhawk fans into a celebratory frenzy.

Barry Sanders shown in December 1998, at the Heisman Reception Ceremony in New York City.

Ron Chismar, former coach at Wichita State University, which killed its program around the same time, had a year or two before he recruited a friend of mine, named Wes Anderson. He was compact and quick like me, but he had battled a string of injuries and wasn't producing enough for Chismar. When asked why he didn't recruit me, Chismar reportedly said, "We don't need another midget."That size thing again, but I'll say this: Coach B showed up big for me.

He created a highlight tape of my season and started lobbying for me. I appreciated it at the time, but his importance has

Barry Sanders is shown with wide receiver Hart Lee Dykes (no. 11) after a game during his junior year at Oklahoma State University.

grown over the years. I had no idea what he went through in advocating for me and I'm not sure where I would have ended up without his efforts.

He called coaches he knew at the various regional programs and pushed my tape. A few times, he said he had to threaten teams that if they didn't return the tape, he'd tell me not to consider the school holding the tape in order to get it back.

I finally decided on Oklahoma State, which had entered the recruiting race late. They were recruiting one of my high school teammates, Joel Fry, who was also quite a wrestler. While watching Joel's highlight reel (where I was featured), the Oklahoma State recruiter wondered who was zipping all over the field behind the blocks. They figured I'd be a good kick returner.

At Oklahoma State, I quickly became my own man. Growing up in a family of 11 kids can make it difficult to find an identity, but I had an apartment, a summer job bagging groceries, and a new and delicious sense of independence. But being your own man, finding yourself and ascending to the next level of maturity can cost a great deal.

In my case, it put me on a collision course with my father. A huge conflict brewed. It began when the OSU recruiting coach came to the house on the day I signed the letter of intent.

Daddy wouldn't speak to the coach, refused to shake his hand and left in anger, saying as he walked out the door, "I think he's making a big mistake." I was hurt by that statement and confused. I didn't know what he meant.

Later, my friend, Mark, said Daddy told him I chose Oklahoma State in order to hide. At OSU, I was playing behind Heisman candidate Thurman Thomas, and I had declined offers from Iowa State and Tulsa, where I would have been the featured back. The conflicts continued after I moved to Stillwater to play for the Cowboys. I was a good and obedient son, but I was also trying to become my own man.

I found myself being forced to choose between my father's wishes, or rather, his commands, and my own sense of what was right and what was reasonable.

Fortunately, Daddy changed his mind. By the time he dropped me off in Stillwater, he supported my decision. He attended all my games, just as he had attended my every sporting event since Little League. He was a strong supporter of the program and of me.

In many ways, it was the happiest time of my life. I was on my own for the first time. I loved the camaraderie and the locker-room atmosphere.

I was comfortable in Thurman's shadow, even though he may not have wanted me there. I had heard that there were scouting reports, warning defensive players against injuring Thurman for fear of having to face me.

If I heard those rumors, I'm sure that he did, too. Those rumors, and his having heard them, actually bothered me, because Thurman was a great back and my teammate.

Soon enough, however, my comfort zone began to collapse. I rushed for 654 yards in 1987, my sophomore season, as Thurman's backup, and I was voted second-team All-American as a kick returner. Thurman earned All-American honors and headed for the NFL, leaving me as the team's featured back. I was moving from the shadows to the spotlight. Toward the Heisman. I'd have to cowboy up, and I did.

THE HEISMAN

The Heisman Trophy was something that I had difficulty understanding. How can you pick one guy and say he's the best? The candidates usually are running backs and quarterbacks, but what about all the down linemen? Those feelings aside, I really did want to win the award. I just didn't want all of the attention that came with it. I love a challenge. I love proving myself.

In 1988, I put together a pretty good season. I broke at least 26 NCAA yardage and scoring records, and I set (and still hold) the season-average records for most rushing yards per game (232), most points per game (21) and most all-purpose yards per game (295). I had two 300-yard games, and 39 touchdowns. No other player in collegiate history at that time had more than one 300-yard game in his career. In that last 300-yard game, I pulled myself out with the single-game collegiate record within reach.

For the season records, I had 600 more yards and 19 more touchdowns than the next person in the record book. I opened two consecutive seasons with a 100-yard kick-off return. I also hold the record for multi-purpose yards in a season. Of course, none of these records would be possible without my teammates. I share accolades with them.

That season was a blur, but so much happened and I'm amazed that many of those records still stand. I held the most yards gained

Barry Sanders is shown at a press conference at the Heisman Reception Ceremony in New York City in December, 1988.

for the season (2,628 yards, with 344 rushes and 11 games) and the most yards gained for the season per game (238.9 yards). I moved into fifth place on the list of earliest games reaching 1,000 yards (1,002 yards).

That same season, I made it to second in most consecutive games gaining 200 yards or more (with five of that season's games), behind the great Marcus Allen, who played for the University of Southern California and had his record-breaking season in 1981.

I still hold the record for most games gaining 300 yards or more for the 1988 season and for my career. I also held the record for most yards gained in three games (937 yards); most yards gained in four games (1,152 yards); and most yards gained in five games (1,472 yards).

On Nov. 5 of that season, a performance by myself and Mike Gaddis of Oklahoma, made us only the second set of opposing Division 1 players to each gain 200 yards or more in a game. I hold the record for most touchdowns scored by rushing in a season (37 rushing touchdowns in 11 games).

Of all those records that season, one that stands out above the rest for me: My brother Byron and I held the record for most yards gained by two brothers in a season—3,690 total yards (I had 2,628 and Byron, who played at Northwestern University, had 1,062 yards).

Despite all of these statistics and records, there were doubters. Michael Wilbon, a sportswriter for the *Washington Post*, for example, told *The Associated Press* he was voting for Rodney Peete of the University of Southern California, or for Steve Walsh of the University of Miami, for the Heisman.

He said that I wasn't one of his top choices, because I hadn't played at the same level of competition. He said my brother, Byron, a 1,000-yard rusher at Northwestern University, could do what I did, had Byron played in the Big 8. "To gain 1,000 yards for Northwestern, you have to be Jim Brown to do that," he said. "I think Byron Sanders, if you switched them, would be identical to Barry."

Comments like that don't bother me. All I care about is my own assessment of my performance.

The announcement of the winner was scheduled for Dec. 4, with the ceremony to be held in New York. I had a choice to make. Attend the ceremony, or stay with my teammates in Tokyo, where we were playing a game against Texas Tech. I chose to stay with the team, and ESPN beamed me into the Downtown Athletic Club for the announcement.

When I heard, "Barry Sanders, of Oklahoma State University," a smile curled on my lips. Though it wasn't in my every waking thought, I really did want the award. After telling the national media that I'd prefer Rodney Peete, my eventual teammate in Detroit, to win the award, I reversed field.

In the game against Texas Tech, I broke the single-season rushing record held by Marcus Allen, who I used to watch on television in awe of his running style. It was a great way to end the regular season. A few weeks later, we met Wyoming at the Holiday Bowl.

Career Rushing Totals at Oklahoma State University

YEAR	ATTEMPTS	YARDS	AVERAGE	TOUCH DOWNS	LONG RUN
1986	74	325	4.4	2	28
1987	105	603	5.7	8	50
1988	344	2,628	7.6	37*	89
TOTAL	523	3,556	6.8	47	89

**He had a total of 39, with a punt return and a kickoff return touchdown.*

Barry Sanders, shown left, is on the sidelines with former Detroit Lions running back Billy Sims, who started his amazing career at the University of Oklahoma, and also won the Heisman Trophy.

At a $175-a-ticket dinner to receive the award, I told a reporter, "I had no idea the things that would follow winning the trophy. I'm happy I did win the award. And if I knew all these things (such as meeting Earl Campbell, Jim Plunkett and Steve Owens) would follow, I might fight Rodney Peete for it."

I was surprised and grateful when I learned of the voting tally. I received 559 of the 721 first-place votes that were cast in the national balloting, eight times as many as Rodney. I finished with 1,878 total points, while Rodney ended up with 912.

Troy Aikman wound up third, with 582. And I did it with no marketing campaign and little national television exposure. In a race dominated by big-school, big-market quarterbacks, I was playing in "an obscure corner of the prairie," in the words of the Washington Post. (I wasn't even on the cover of the Oklahoma State football program. I didn't appear in the book until page 22.) Still, I didn't put myself in the same category as past winners, such as Billy Sims, Tony Dorsett, Marcus Allen and Charles White. But everyone else did, and my stock was suddenly soaring.

ON TO THE NFL

I really wanted to return to Oklahoma State for my senior year. As I said earlier, I was very happy there. It was fun being in college, and I wasn't ready to leave it behind yet. I had been the featured back for only one year. I wanted to stay. That's what Mother wanted, too.

But the NCAA hammer was dropping on Oklahoma State for a variety of violations, which allowed me to leave early. Others were telling me that I needed to enter the draft, in order to maximize my earning potential. It was a tough decision to make.

Perhaps the worst of all, I got my first taste of what was to come in my relationship with my father. During the press conference, at which I announced that I'd be staying in school, despite the NCAA sanctions, Mother told a reporter, "It would be his money anyway, as far as I'm concerned. I feel it is necessary to finish one thing before you go onto something else. That's important to me. And I think if there is money this year, surely there will be some next year also."

To which Daddy responded: "I'm not as broad-minded as Shirley. She's talking about his money. I say our money, because I'm going to be one of his principal agents."

As my deadline for declaring for the draft approached, I got another dose of what was to come in my relationship with my father. I listened to Daddy for hours, literally hours, scream and curse at me for even considering a return for my senior year in Stillwater. I'd never seen him so emotional.

I folded.

Before I knew it, I was making that long drive to Denver for another press conference, this time to announce my plan to enter the NFL draft, and to preside over the official end of my childhood.

CHAPTER SIX

The Rookie

Entering the NFL was like entering a small room full of gunfire, or like being trapped on the median of a 75-mile-per-hour highway.

On April 24, 1989, the Detroit Lions chose me in the first round, with the third pick in the draft, and I officially became a professional football player. But I didn't sign a contract until Sept. 8. The season opened a few days later, and since I'd sat out all of training camp, I wasn't prepared. I got my first whiff of what I'd face in the next 10 years, in the first game against the Phoenix Cardinals. We were trailing late in the third quarter, when Coach Wayne Fontes sent me into the game. My first run as a professional went for 18 yards.

Running a variation of only one play, I finished the day with 71 rushing yards and a touchdown on nine carries. It was a good start, but while out on the field, the differences between the college and the pro game shocked me.

In college, you might face a defense with a couple of players with pro-grade speed, but in the NFL, everyone is world-class. Everyone, from the strong safety to the 300-pound lineman, moves quickly. In that first game, it seemed like bodies were whizzing by me like bullets and colliding like cymbals.

> No one in their right mind would throw themselves off a roof, over and over and over again, and yet, that's what we did to our bodies once a week, nine months a year, until we left the game, or until the game left us.

In what was then the NFC Central Division, I spent a lot of time on artificial turf. The pounding my knees took on that turf, frequently caused them to swell, and the surface—basically pavement covered by a thin, green rug—potato-peeled my forearms. My running still saved me from a lot of the calamitous shots that some backs and receivers took, but I did take a shot against the Bears in the third game of my rookie season that sidelined me with bruised ribs.

It felt great to be a professional player, a member of the NFL, but that was never my dream—not even close. When I was young, I wondered if I was good enough to play college ball, and even then, I just wanted to be competitive.

I never thought I would stand out. Moving into pro ball, I felt the same way. I wanted to know if I could compete—not necessarily excel—on that level. Being there fed my natural curiosity as much as anything. I had always loved football, and now I was a screaming groupie, suddenly allowed backstage.

I do think, though, that making it to pro ball was one of my brother's dreams.

CRUELLY CLOSE

One day, Byron is in the spotlight as the star running back of Northwestern University, only the third player at the school to run for 1,000 yards in a season, in the rugged Big 10 Conference. His name and face are all over the pages of the Tribune and the Sun-Times sports sections. He's drafted by the Chicago Bears and signs a two-year contract. He's so close to his dream.

But then the Bears cut him.

Only a few months removed from the wide streets of Chicago and all of that attention, he was back home in Wichita in his old room, grieving for the apparent end of his dream. I'm convinced that his collision with that fate was more violent than any he would have had to absorb in the league. It was a disappointment far deeper than most of us will ever experience.

I say that, because so few of us get as cruelly and tantalizingly close to our dreams as Byron got to his, only to watch it dissolve. And he wasn't one of those empty dreamers, either.

> Too many people have dreams, but place them on a shelf and stare at them longingly. Helplessly. They never put in the work that might bring the dream to life.

That's not true of my brother. He followed a muscle-bursting weight program. He jogged. He ran sprints. He studied nutrition and ate balanced meals. He ran stadium stairs. He maintained an impressive level of fitness year-round, and had done so for as long as I can remember. He wanted it so badly.

And it looked like he was going to get it. After graduating from North, Byron went to Hutchinson Community College for two years, and then sat out a year, because of a knee injury.

He then transferred to Northwestern University and gained 1,062 yards, tying Mike Adamle's school rushing record. Rather than return for his senior season, he wanted to turn pro, which he now feels may have been a mistake.

Barry Sanders is shown with coach Wayne Fontes his rookie year playing for the Detroit Lions as a running back.

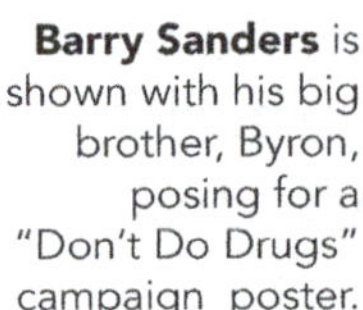

Barry Sanders is shown with his big brother, Byron, posing for a "Don't Do Drugs" campaign poster.

Despite his success at Northwestern, the Bears waited until the ninth round to take him, with the 248th overall pick in the 1989 draft. A few weeks into training camp, they let him go. At the time, he felt that he never really got a chance to prove himself. As time passed, he wondered if he wasn't ready, if he should have stayed for another season at Northwestern to prepare himself for pro ball. A few years after the Bears cut him, Byron got a tryout with the Lions and with the World Football League, but he was cut again.

I could see the repercussions of that disappointment rippling through his life as the years passed. First, he went back to college, where he earned a degree in human development and social policy from Northwestern, in 1992. After graduation, he searched for a career that would make him happy. But some college stars who don't make it in the pros take a few years to find their footing.

He worked a two-year stint in Wichita as the head coach for a small Christian high school. He really seemed to grow within that role, but after that job, he still seemed lost. Even while he was at the high school, his teams played games at the Little League field named after me. But Byron has always been as compassionate as he is passionate. As a coach, he pushed the kids to push themselves, but he'd also drive to their homes to help them with their homework. In that way, he was the helpful, gently guiding big brother Byron I'd always known.

You might think differently, but he never seemed bothered about the perception that he lived in my shadow. I think he has always been happy for me. I also think, however, that not casting a shadow of his own did hurt him. I have to say, it was difficult for me, too, not simply because I care for him, but because I've always been his biggest fan. I feel as if I share in his disappointments.

When we were children, I followed him from the basketball courts to the football fields and back. I wanted to do everything he did, and when my friends would invite me to places, I'd always ask if Byron could come along. It was a great moment when Wichita North retired my football jersey and retired Byron's, too.

Except for my parents and for my sister, Nancy, Byron influenced me more than anyone else in my family. We were particularly close, because of our ages. He's just a year older than me. We have an older brother, Boyd, but he had moved out of the house by the time Byron and I were teenagers, and so we were the only boys in a house with eight sisters. During my early years in the NFL, Byron came to live with me. He seemed to be trying to find his way.

FIRST STUTTER-STEPS

If Byron's career was over, mine was just beginning. The on-field challenges intrigued and excited me, but the off-field challenges bored and frustrated me. Off the field, there were times when I felt that I didn't belong in the league. I signed autographs out of obligation, but I neither understood, nor enjoyed it. I did like the handshakes and the photographs and the polite patter with the fans, especially children, but I was so green that I hadn't learned yet how to say, "Okay, I've signed enough of these. I need to get home or to practice." I hated disappointing people, but I hated even more the sense that I could never get away.

Worse, I was learning lessons about the financial predators who target pro athletes. Try thinking this way: When you enter a crowded room, all you can see is the crowd. But you learn to consider the crowd as foliage or brush, helping to conceal an attack in the form of a confidence scheme. Let's just say that many times when someone is patting you on the back, they aren't congratulating you, they're trying to get you to cough up something—like money.

On the field, it was much different. I spent much of that first season dealing with a couple of nagging injuries, particularly a hip pointer that I suffered against the Bears. I had to play catch-up for most of the season when it came to learning the playbook—a phonebook-thick encyclopedia of our basic plays, sets and philosophy. Having missed all of training camp, I was behind everyone else learning the system.

At that time, the Lions used a complicated offensive attack called the Silver Stretch. The Silver Stretch was the pro version of an offense called the Run and Shoot, which was used by a couple of college teams. In that offense, the object was to spread out the defenders and attack them with quick passes to speedy receivers, or use draw plays by the running back before the defense had a chance to react. All that space created by the spread-open defense, gave me room to operate, to make people miss and to rack up yardage.

The season took an interesting path. I didn't have a 100-yard game until the third game of the season, when we played the Bears. I had 126 yards on 18 carries, in a little more than one-half of the game. Two games later, I gained 99 yards against the Vikings, making so many guys miss tackles that their coach, Jerry Burns, asked officials to check my jersey. He thought I sprayed it with silicon so no one could grab it.

I went off for 184 yards on 30 carries against Green Bay, and on Thanksgiving Day, I broke the 1,000-yard mark, by gaining 145 yards against Cleveland.

I think I earned a ceremonial turkey leg for that performance, from TV analyst and former coach John Madden. Later in the year, I broke the rookie record for yards gained in a season, a record held by a former Lion, who also had worn number 20: Billy Sims. Billy was at the game to congratulate me on the field, a great honor.

I received a number of honors for that first year: I was named first-team All Pro by *The Associated Press*, *The Sporting News*, the *Pro Football Writers of America*, *Football Digest* and *College & Pro Football News Weekly*. A number of those publications and organizations, as well as a number of others, named me the NFL Rookie of the Year. I also made my first trip to the Pro Bowl.

I was fortunate to achieve so much success and must credit God and my teammates. I really wasn't aiming that high. I only wanted to be competitive.

The Detroit Lions No. 20s are shown, from left, Barry Sanders, Billy Sims and Lem Barney.

CHAPTER SEVEN

Nancy

The toughest person I've ever known wasn't Daddy, and it wasn't Lawrence Taylor, Howie Long or John Lynch. The toughest person I've ever known was my sister, Nancy. And the toughest thing I've ever had to endure was watching her fight a slow death. No one teaches you how to deal with something like that. You can't prepare for it. As we all do, I had to learn as I went, and even then I found myself wondering how there could be so much pain in the world.

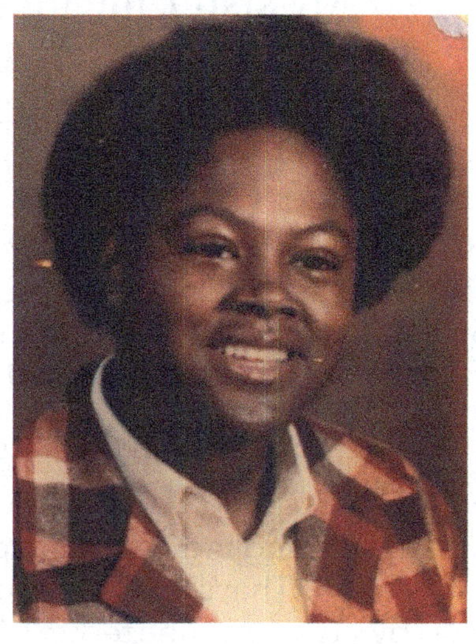

Nancy Sanders is shown while attending Wichita State University, after graduating from Emporia State University.

The disease that killed Nancy is called scleroderma, a despicable condition that hardens and scars skin and connective tissue. It is one of a group of arthritic conditions with no known cause or cure. An estimated 300,000 people in the United States suffer from this condition, nearly four times more women than men. As it progressed in Nancy, we watched helplessly, as if watching a burning house collapse around her; only in her case, the house was her own body.

I watched this slow-motion implosion over the span of several years. With Nancy, the disease began with what we thought were only patches of stubbornly dry skin. But soon, those patches began to get thicker and harder, and they started to spread to her hands, arms, face and neck. Then they started to scar and discolor.

Doctors say that there are two major forms of the disease: One form primarily affects the skin. The other, though, launches an all-out attack on not only the skin, but also on the lungs, the kidneys and the gastrointestinal tract. Scleroderma leaves a person freezer-burned, inside and out.

My sister meant the world to me, and calling her "sister" doesn't capture her role in my life, or her place in my heart. She was my sister, my mama and my friend.

Helplessly watching her suffer through the roller coaster of remission and collapse was perhaps the most agonizing episode of my life. The disease rotted her joints and inflamed them, making movement often blindingly painful.

It hardened her intestines to the point that she couldn't absorb nutrients, starving her. It hardened her lungs so she couldn't breathe, strangling her. Most people fear drowning, because of suffocation. That's what this anaconda of a disease did to Nancy; little by little, it squeezed the life out of her.

But Nancy always seemed to have a quality that transcended life.

MEMORIES OF NANCY

I have a fond early memory, of going with Mother to pick up Nancy from elementary school. She didn't go to the school we all attended, or would attend when we were older. Most parents have to request that their child be tested as gifted and talented, but Nancy bloomed so brightly in the meadow of students that her teachers felt compelled to move her into a more challenging school.

Her accomplishments in school meant a great deal to me. It gave me an inner glow that she was such a good student, and made me feel special that she was so special. She always seemed to go out of her way to make me feel important. She'd decorate the house, for example, and throw birthday parties for me, and I don't remember her doing that for anyone else in the

The Sanders family is shown in the spring 1991. Pictured in the back row, are Boyd, Deddy, Mother and Byron; in the middle row, are Barry, Elaine, Gloria, Nancy and Diane; and in the front row, are Donna, Gina, Lynn and Krista.

family. After my high school football games, she'd rally the family to paint banners and organize family parades for me.

Nancy always seemed to be there when I needed her. When I was about three years old, Mother took Nancy and me on a ride to where my daddy worked, to bring him lunch. I was in Nancy's lap. Mother said when she turned a corner, the door of our old station wagon flew open, and Nancy and I were jolted out into the street. Either from fear or from pure instinct, Nancy wrapped me in a bear hug and made sure that when we hit the pavement, I landed on her. Mother says Nancy saved my life.

I always felt good being around Nancy, because she exuded a limitless capacity for giving. She was always working on some sketch, school project or church function. She was always trying to help people and to make herself a better person. She loved to sing, whether it was an aria from an opera, or stirring gospel hymns. She loved to dance. She loved to sew her own clothes.

And she loved to laugh. She always seemed to be trying to make other people laugh, too. Her skits and imitations—inspired by Jerry Lewis and Gilda Radner—were rockets of creativity. We all laughed, especially when she imitated Daddy. But Radner was one of her particular favorites. I'd stay up with her to watch Radner on Saturday Night Live. Nancy's favorite character on the show was Radner's Rosanne Rosannadanna. I really didn't understand the show or the comedy; I just enjoyed hanging with her.

I remember one night, I was flipping channels and caught a

glimpse of Gilda Radner biography—and burst into tears. When I saw Radner's image floating on the screen, I lost it.

The image brought back many memories of Nancy, her creativity and her humor—her wonderful spirit. It also brought back the pain of watching one of the strongest people I've ever known being driven down, down, down by an incurable disease.

She was trapped in a deteriorating body, and even with all of my muscles and money, I could do nothing, but watch. The fingers that filled our house with piano music, were now stiffened, wracked with pain.

The arms that held me when we tumbled from the car were often folded uselessly in her lap. The person who'd boldly hung "No Smoking" signs in the house (a not-so-subtle suggestion to Daddy and his cigars), and taught me about the importance of standing up for myself, found it physically painful to stand up. It was tough watching life so cruelly stolen from someone who not only wanted to give, but who also had so much to give.

Despite what happened to her and the way she suffered, I can't feel sad without feeling as if I'm betraying her somehow. She would want me to be strong, to move forward.

Nancy spent much of the last year of her life with me in Detroit, moving into my place in the summer of 1991. She'd already been ill for some time, but I didn't know much about the disease, and asked her once, somewhat offhandedly, about the odds that she would overcome it.

"Fifty-fifty," she said. At that moment, I felt a creeping fear rise from my stomach to my throat.

Despite those odds, she handled herself with her usual courage. She enrolled at Langston (Oklahoma) University, in a master's of music program. Langston is considered a Historically Black College or University (HBCU). That took a lot of guts, because little by little, I could see the disease chipping away at her.

She could still drive, but walking became difficult. She tired easily. The pain was getting worse.

But she handled it so well. She didn't want anyone to feel sorry for her, and she wouldn't let anyone do anything for her that she could do herself. She knew she was going to die, but she said that if she died later rather than sooner, she'd have her master's degree in music.

She was so strong. It was as if she were fighting off the deliberate march of the disease, in order to give all of us time to come to terms with it, understand it and say our good-byes.

She drove home to Wichita from Langston one weekend, not feeling well. When she arrived, she felt worse, and my sisters called for an ambulance.

She died at the hospital.

I was preparing for a game in Tampa Bay against the Buccaneers, when my little sister, Krista, called to tell me that Nancy had died. I remember thinking to myself, in the midst of the pain of losing her: Could you have done more? Surely, there was something else you could have done. But then I thought: She wouldn't have let me do more. It wasn't worth dwelling on anyway. It's better to remember her zest for life.

My appreciation for the arts comes from Nancy, too. Every time I've seen a play, I've thought of her. She always saw me as being someone better than I thought I could be. Had she been with me, I'd laughed a lot more over the years. I'd probably be a little wiser. I'm sure I'd be a better person.

But I can't be sad about the 27 years of her life, much of which I got to experience. It was a gift, a blessing, a joy and a privilege. I was fortunate to be her brother. A newspaper reporter wrote in Nancy's obituary that William Sanders said if you think his son is tough, you should have known his daughter, Nancy.

How true.

CHAPTER EIGHT

The Roar Restored

Success often seems to arrive, in spite of something, and often on the far end of probability. You win, sometimes, in spite of injuries. You win, in spite of controversy that threatens team focus. You win, in spite of general adversity.

In 1991, our team had all three, but we fell just one game short of the Super Bowl. We closed the season with a record of 12-4, nearly achieving what Coach Fontes imagined when he began his plan to "Restore the Roar" in Detroit. It was the most exciting year of my career. I never would have guessed that things would have turned out that way, given how badly things began.

I'll explain.

Shortly after the 1990 season ended, I'd asked the Lions to restructure and renegotiate my contract, and the situation began rotting from there. The Lions resisted, and I dug in, too. Month after month passed without a resolution. As the '91 season approached, it appeared that I'd be holding out of training camp.

In the meantime, I was being sued for a business investment involving a highway truck stop in Kansas. When the plan soured, everyone started looking for someone to sue, and before I knew anything, everyone was looking at me.

I sat out nearly the entire training camp before settling my contract dispute, and then I badly bruised my ribs in a preseason game with the Kansas City Chiefs. By the time our opener against the Washington Redskins rolled around, my ribs were so sore, I could barely run. I couldn't twist my trunk at all without a belt of pain squeezing the breath out of me.

I sat out the game, and it appeared that the rest of the team did, too. We lost 45-0, our worst defeat since Dallas pounded us 59-13 in 1968, the year I was born.

Coach Fontes shagged the questions reporters threw at him about my injury. "He told the coaches he was tightening up during the pregame meal, and I watched him work out prior to the game," Wayne told the press. "He was running gingerly, and he decided he couldn't go."

I guess the questions persisted, because he then added, "I think Barry is a tough back, but any player who tells me he can't play, then I won't play him. Barry is a unique talent, and the season isn't going to be won or lost in one game."

The timing, of course, could not have been worse. I was fresh off a hold-out, and then I sat out a game in which we posted an historic loss to open the season. I also began to hear whispers about my toughness.

But winning is the antidote to just about any set of problems that might face a professional football team. We went out and won the next five games, going into the bye week at 5-1. After the week off, our fortunes went up and down. We lost, then

Former Detroit Lions player Mike Utley is shown on the field awaiting a stretcher to take him off the field.

won, then lost two more. Our problem mostly stemmed from injuries. As the season progressed, we lost starting quarterback Rodney Peete, linebacker Mike Cofer, nose guard Jerry Ball, as well as two linemen, Mike Utley and Eric Sanders.

THUMBS UP

Losing Mike Utley was the most frightening experience I'd ever had on a football field. It happened during our Nov. 17 home game against the Los Angeles Rams. During a play, Mike fell forward, and the top of his helmet got caught on the turf, cracking his neck. His spinal cord was damaged beyond repair.

> We didn't know the seriousness or the nature of his injury at the time. We all just stood there, eyes wide, breathing softly and waiting impatiently for him to get up.

It seemed like we stood there for an hour. Before long, players from both teams had joined hands, knelt right there on the field and prayed. A nervous murmur vibrated through the crowd, as emergency medical staff hovered over him. I'd always said, even in college, that all of my success could end in one play. Mike's injury was the first time I'd actually seen anything close to that happen.

As he was being wheeled away to applause, he raised his thumb, detonating a wild burst of cheers that literally turned the season around. We went on to beat the Rams that day, 21-10, and we won the next five games to finish the season at 12-4, the franchise's best record since a Lions team went 11-3, back in 1962.

The team I played on in my first season was pretty good, and we won some games, ending up with a record of 7-9. Those numbers may not sound great, but we had finished well, winning six of our final seven games—the final five in a row—and so in my second season, we were supposed to be pretty good. But we didn't play that well, ending up at 6-10.

Then, in that magical third season, we just got hot. We had a good combination of strengths. We had young guys who had a lot of fire. We had great special teams, and we had a good defense and an explosive offense. Seven players on that team were elected at the end of the season to play in the Pro Bowl: Jerry Ball, Bennie Blades, Lomas Brown, Mel Gray, Chris Spielman and yours truly.

I think we had been waiting on that team to show up for the first couple of years, and in '91 it finally came together. We dedicated our season to Mike. We used his thumbs-up signal as our rallying point, and went on to win the NFC Central Division title. We hosted and won our first playoff game in years by blasting the talented, but rebuilding Dallas Cowboys 38-6. I don't think we realized we were capable of such a game. If we did realize it, we certainly had never witnessed it. We ran the ball, we passed the ball and the defense dominated.

We were a hair's breadth from the Super Bowl. We needed to win only one more game. Unfortunately, we needed to win it against the Washington Redskins. The Redskins were awesome that year. They finished at 14-2, the best record in the league. They led the league in points scored, and only the Saints had given up fewer points. The Redskins had annihilated us in the season opener. In the NFC Championship, it was just about as ugly as the first game.

I had 44 yards on six carries in the first quarter of that game, and was forced to stay in the backfield and block Washington's blitzing linebackers. In the remaining three quarters, things got even worse. We fell behind 10-0 in the first four minutes of the game, and trailed 17-10 at halftime.

In the third quarter, the dam burst, literally and figuratively. We played in a cold, heavy rain, and our offense couldn't get untracked in the sucking mud, while the Redskins ran wind sprints through our defense.

I finished the day with 44 yards on 11 carries. And it wasn't as if I wasn't trying. On one run, I ran close to 80 yards for a simple 6-yard gain, running sideline to sideline.

Barry Sanders is shown giving a press conference after the Restore the Roar event.

"We had to work for everything we got," I told reporters after the game. And we didn't get much. The 41-10 loss disappointed us, but we lost to a great team. The Redskins went on to whip the Buffalo Bills in the Super Bowl, a game my teammates and I had to watch on television like everybody else.

In later years, we'd show flashes of that team's talent and chemistry, but it would never quite come together the way it did in 1991. We'd have an explosive offense and a marginal defense, or a stingy defense and a plodding offense. Never both.

We also had more than our share of tragedies. Mike Utley would never play again. In June 1992, a talented young lineman named Eric Andolsek was killed in a freak accident, when a sleeping truck driver ran off the road and into Eric's front yard, running him down. Five years later, linebacker Reggie Brown would suffer a paralyzing spinal injury.

That NFL championship game was as close as I ever got to a Super Bowl in my 10 years in the league.

WORDS FROM LOMAS BROWN FORMER TEAMMATE, DETROIT LIONS

The year we had in 1991 was great, especially the way the team overcame the tragedy of Mike Utley's injury. That brought us together. In a way, the season just magically happened. We were young, and I guess we didn't know any better, and Wayne was the perfect coach.

But the key was Barry. Without the threat of Barry Sanders, teams would have been bringing the house at us. But they couldn't come at us so hard with him in there, because they had to try to contain him. If I get into the Hall of Fame, it's because of him. He made it easier to keep my guy off the line.

At the same time, it was hard to block for Barry, because you didn't know where he was going to be. I might be assigned as the back-side tackle on a play, but then Barry would reverse field and go the other way, so I'd have to scramble and be the front-side guy. He wouldn't always go to the hole where you thought he was going. But when he had the ball in his hand, there was always a possibility he was going all the way, and we knew that when we were blocking for him.

The team was more like family than any other one I was ever on. We opened our houses to each other, gave each other advice and really cared about each other. That chemistry was one of the reasons we were good. And everybody loved Barry. But when you invited him for dinner, look out. He could eat.

One time, he came over to my house with some Dove bars and polished three or four of them. Then my wife fixed him a full plate of food, and he ate that, too. My daughters' mouths were hanging open from watching him. He was a machine.

He could sleep, too. I used to tell him he had a sleeping disorder. Once he fell asleep on the sideline during a game. He was sleeping with his helmet on.

I told him that's why he started wearing that visor, so he could sleep on the bench and no one would know. He'd do that in meetings, too. As soon as the lights went off, Barry's head would start to nod. But he was able to get away with it.

Of course, he could have gotten away with a lot more. He was a superstar, but he didn't ever use that to get his way. He was a good person, a Christian, a lot like his mother. Jerry Ball and I used to say, "God blessed the right man. He knew who to give it to." If we'd had as much power as B (which is what we called him) we wouldn't have handled it as well as he did. Sometimes, I wished he would have been more outspoken. We could have gotten a lot more done there with management.

Chuck Schmidt, the general manager, didn't like when players tried to use their power. He felt threatened. That's why management ended up getting rid of so many guys on the team—Mel Gray, Bennie Blades, Jerry Ball, Chris Spielman, Brett Perriman, Willie Green, some others. Chuck was like that. But management knew Barry wasn't going to make any waves. He was so quiet and didn't seem threatening to anybody.

It's a shame they started tearing down that team. That playoff game in '91 shows you what we could have done. We beat Dallas, dismantled them, and they were similar to us. We were both young and building something. They went up from there, and where did we go? We could have won a Super Bowl. We could have won a couple times. When I won the Super Bowl with Tampa Bay, I thought about all of those guys: Barry, Bennie, Kevin Glover and the rest of them. I thought about what we could have done.

The 1991 Season Week by Week

Week	Opponent	Result	Score
1	at Washington Redskins	L	0-45
2	Green Bay Packers	W	23-14
3	Miami Dolphins	W	17-13
4	at Indianapolis Colts	W	33-24
5	Tampa Bay Buccaneers	W	31-3
6	Minnesota Vikings	W	24-20
7	BYE WEEK		
8	at San Francisco 49ers	L	3-35
9	Dallas Cowboys	W	34-10
10	at Chicago Bears	L	10-20
11	at Tampa Bay Buccaneers	L	21-30
12	Los Angeles Rams	W	21-10
13	at Minnesota Vikings	W	34-14
14	Chicago Bears	W	16-6
15	New York Jets	W	34-20
16	at Green Bay Packers	W	21-17
17	at Buffalo Bills	W	17-14

POSTSEASON

NFC Division Playoff			
	Dallas Cowboys	W	38-6
NFC Championship Game			
	at Washington Redskins	L	10-41

CHAPTER NINE

An Uneasy Crown

It was as if the wide-eyed boy had driven his little toes through the tile floor of the grocery store. His mother tugged and pulled at him, but she might as well have been pulling on a fire hydrant.

Barry Sanders being interviewed.

The boy had spotted me.

I had just received a hero's welcome in Wichita that day as the city's first and only Heisman Trophy winner. There was a parade, rallies and gifts from the mayor, including a key to the city. And when it finally was over, all I wanted to do was stop by a store and buy some Suzy Q's.

But as I was walking into the store, I noticed the little boy, who seemed to know who I was. He also seemed nervous, so I walked over and grabbed his hand and pumped it as if I was his biggest fan.

I said, 'Hey, how are you doing? I've always wanted to meet you!"

The boy, his mouth slightly open, stared. He looked confused, but excited. He smiled, probably because he couldn't manage to actually say anything.

I poured it on and asked for his autograph.

We found a pen and a couple of pieces of paper and the boy started writing, spending several seconds on each letter. His mother smiled. I don't think she knew who I was, but seemed to be touched by the gentle attention I gave her son. The boy finished, smiled and started to walk away,

Then I asked, "Do you think you'd like my autograph?"

The boy smiled again, slightly embarrassed. I gave him my autograph and he walked away grinning and looking up at his mother. I don't think he ever managed to say a word, except maybe a thank you.

It's funny, but as naturally as that exchange came for me, and with all of the time I spent in front of cameras and microphones, I always found dealing with people to be the most difficult task I had as a player. I was uncomfortable signing autographs. When someone approaches, I feel as if I'm suddenly the center of attention.

I appreciate the fans and feel grateful that they're interested in me, but when I'm out with my family or friends, it's hard to shift roles, to be an average person one minute and in the spotlight the next.

But the more successful I became, the more I had to deal with (or try to avoid) the media, and the more autographs I was being asked to sign. For a while, I'd sign them and include a Bible verse. But eventually, I got to the point where I would try not to sign any, opting for a photograph or even a handshake.

I've learned to enjoy my freedom and at times, my anonymity. When I'm out in public, invariably, someone will walk up and say that I look like Barry Sanders, often adding, "but you're too small to be him."

Fame changed every relationship I'd ever had, except for the one with my mother. Everyone changed. At times, it was frustrating. Other times, it was maddening. Most of the time, it was just lonely.

I was one of a handful notable athletes with a squeaky-clean image. The problem with such images is that they are static. They don't allow for growth or maturity. Growing up in Kansas and going to college in Oklahoma, I entered the league about as green and as earnest as a young man could be. On campus, when people would ask where I planned to go when I finished there, I told them, "I want to go to heaven."

In the league, I had to grow up quickly, and I found out quickly that players on the field were warriors, but off the field, we were the prey of everyday scammers and hustlers.

After just a year of dealing with them, I longed to face the fire-breathing linemen and linebackers on the football field who wanted to tear my head off. At least they honor certain rules and boundaries. At least they don't follow you home. At least they don't ring your phone incessantly.

Despite the fact that my wife at the time and my best friend are journalists, their world of words and images remains a mystery to me. When I came into the league, I did interviews sparingly, not knowing that when it comes to the media, you can run, but you can't hide. I'm the type of player who does his talking on the field, not in the locker room.

> I deliver my message through the way I play, and I assumed that approach would be enough for people. I hadn't learned yet that when you're quiet, you forfeit your right to fairness and self-definition.

If you don't talk, the media will talk for you. Then again, if I knew that, I may have talked even less. I'm no expert, but I think people in the media create these caricatures for a couple of reasons.

First, subjects and sources have to fit neatly into stereotypes for easy packaging, so I became the, "Aw shucks, Midwestern Bible boy," someone easy for readers/viewers to recognize in the brief moments reporters have to hook them.

Second, it is also easier to do superficial stories than to do the intense reporting necessary to find out what really makes people tick, what experiences have broken their hearts and what inspires them. You have to get close to them and talk to them, and at the same time, you have to give a little bit of yourself in the process.

That kind of intense reporting doesn't happen very much, and I'll admit to not trusting people enough to let it happen.

THE HUNT AND THE HUNTED

After we've been reduced to mere caricatures—no longer people with lives, emotions and loved ones—the hunt escalates. I can recall trying to enjoy a night with my wife, not long after I announced my retirement.

Our evening was interrupted when glaring lights and probing cameras showed up outside the venue. Some nut had started what amounted to a "Find Barry" contest. If you saw me (and their cameras always spotted me eventually) then you won $50. This contest apparently was meant to hound me back onto the team.

Antics such as that contest caused me to be reluctant to go out in public. After announcing my retirement, I just didn't want to deal with the fall-out among the media and the fans. So I headed for London. But while the plane was still sitting on the tarmac, hoards of journalists, moving like groaning zombies, were trying to board. I can't tell you how concerned I was as we sat there, and how relieved I was when the flight attendants finally closed the doors.

I've always wondered how journalists would feel if athletes could somehow find a way to rate them, day in and day out, hound them in their personal lives, and even call for their firing or removal. What if we kept track of all the corrections, typos and grammar busts that creep into their copy? I can only hope that someday, we'll find a way. I may sound bitter, but I'm really not. As I said, some of my best friends are journalists.

After some time away from the spotlight, I've been able to put all of this attention into perspective. I remember HBO inviting me to a televised fight held in Detroit's Joe Louis Arena. I told them I couldn't make it, but for some reason, my response didn't get to the announcers. They announced to the crowd I was there.

People booed my name with the enthusiasm they used to cheer for me from the stands. It was disappointing, but I also looked at it as sort of a compliment. I felt as though they still wanted to see me play. They weren't happy I retired. They wanted me back on the field, and the booing was a window into their disappointment.

People enjoyed what I did, and I'm at peace with that.

CHAPTER TEN

Splendor on the Grass

Anyone who has ever done anything astounding, started with a vision of what he or she wanted to create. That vision begins with a picture you play over and over in your mind. For me, the vision formed on fall Saturday afternoons, while watching Tony Dorsett, the University of Pittsburgh's amazing running back, pierce the line and rocket down the sideline. It formed on Sunday afternoons when I saw Marcus Allen gliding like a figure skater over the turf.

After watching them, I would run outside and recreate the scenes in the front yard, imagining myself making the moves and running the way I'd seen those great players do it. I would create the vision as precisely as possible. Then I would open my eyes.

It was a dream so real, I could almost touch the grass. Taste the sweet air. Feel the texture of the ball. Running the football was something almost spiritual for me. It was the first thing I ever paid close attention to as a kid, the first thing that caught my eye about the game of football.

I have always loved basketball, especially dribbling past a defender and dunking or flicking a jumper over someone's outstretched hand.

As a kid, I spent hours at recess playing soccer. I used to love to watch Sugar Ray Leonard shower his opponents with shots that landed like steel raindrops. But football always was my favorite sport.

No play in football is like a nice long run. Every facet of the act fascinated me: running through the line; making people miss. I wanted to do it. And I wanted to do it in the way I envisioned. To witness that live, to see it happening before your eyes, is incredible. It took me to another world. I saw what I wanted to do in Tony D. and Marcus Allen. Marcus didn't just run the ball. He looked graceful. He moved me.

I remember people talking about how NBA-great Larry Bird prepared for games. A couple of hours before tip-off, Larry was already facing the defenders in his mind. He'd lower his shoulder and drive toward the man, pressing him onto his heels, then pull up for the fade away. He'd back his man in, and then spin to the board with a finger-roll. He'd chase a ball out of bounds, leap, snag the ball and turn in mid-air to fire a shot from behind the backboard that splashed through the net.

During the game, it may have looked like Larry was improvising, especially that behind-the-backboard shot that dropped all net. But those are things he had practiced, or at least thought about or that he had prepared himself to do. It was the first time the scrambling defender had seen the scenario, but Larry had replayed those scenes in his mind over and over. You've got to have such a vision.

I had a vision, too, and it was beautiful. I put everything I was into it. Loving it dragged me into the weight room to lift weights until my arms burned, and it dragged me to run steep mountain slopes during the off-season, until my lungs crackled. It made me prepare. It made me dream about what I might do next.

HOW (NOT) TO CARRY THE FOOTBALL

Football is about forward progress. You get three chances to move the ball 10 yards through a human wall dug in to stop you. If you don't make it in those three chances, you kick the ball away from the goal you're defending, and your opponent then tries to run through your human wall. Walls collide again and again in the fight for yardage. As the team plows forward—north and south, straight ahead—every inch counts. You keep your legs driving.

Moving backward is anathema. In fact, teams are penalized for infractions by being moved away from their goal. Yardage, football's currency, gets swapped on every play. Stopping, jumping, moving from side to side, and especially reversing field and running backward, gives that wall of defenders time to fight through your wall and mob you for a loss. You lost yardage. Runners are taught from their infancy to avoid these temptations. But laws are made to be broken, and I broke virtually all of the rules of carrying the ball.

On any given play, I'd stop my feet. I'd jump. I'd dance side to side in the narrow paths that form between those two crashing walls. I'd sometimes run backward. Angelo Dundee, Mohammad Ali's legendary trainer, once said that the champ, "did everything wrong, but it turned out right." People have said that I did everything wrong, but it turned out right—sometimes.

IN THE MOMENT

Take the pitch and tuck the ball tightly
in the crook of your arm. Float to the right,
following the blockers. Eyes up.
Control your speed—then ... bam! Punch a hole in
the line. Defenders fly at you like snowflakes, but you
ski around them, sliding down a green mountainside.
More arrive, others follow.
You stop and they run past. You plant right, wait for
them to run there, and then burst left, their hands
snatching air and their facemasks mowing grass. Suddenly, the field opens, and you're alone with the sound
of your rhythmic breathing and thudding heartbeat.
No crowd, no coaches, no teammates.
The bouncing landscape looms larger ahead of you.
Your cleats don't seem to be touching the ground.
Legs burning, chest on fire. The goal line. A flood of
sounds. Cheering. Whistles. Teammates.

I would often lose ground with the chances I took by stopping, spinning, jumping and reversing field. But I was adhering to a much more important rule. A long time ago, Daddy told me to run like a scared rabbit, so that's what I did. I figured the only rule that mattered was the one that said, Don't Get Tackled.

Perhaps my favorite such run came when I was a freshman in college in a game against Houston. It wasn't a long run—something like 11 yards. I didn't even score. But it was special. I remember dancing around the backfield and changing directions. I remember guys falling around me, and it was almost like I was controlling them, controlling their movements.

As a player, I lived for the compressed excitement of those moments, the moments when people stand up and stop breathing as they watch. They aren't cheering yet, but the anticipation, the possibility, pulls them to their feet. It's the same kind of startled excitement you feel for a split second when you catch yourself falling over backward in a chair. I wanted to exist within those moments, play in those moments, ignite those moments.

I don't think I could have been as successful a runner if I had followed the rules and plunged right into the chests of defenders. That approach only would have made it easier for them to catch me.

Before the start of training camp one year, the coaches showed the team a highlight tape of the history of the franchise. The tape included a 13-yard touchdown run I made against Green Bay in 1994. I started right, doubled back to the left, stopped and cut back three more times. Nine of the 11 Packer defenders hit me during the run—pad-on-pad shots that could have resulted in tackles—but none of them brought me down. The Packers had many excellent players, and I was fortunate to elude them. Touchdown.

It's possible to make a lot of people miss you with this running style. The longer you're on your feet, the better your chance at scoring. One run against Chicago was a prime example. It was just an off-tackle play to the right. I remember thinking this would be an average run, a couple of yards, if that far. But then, I remember running into defenders and we kind of bounced outside.

I remember they started falling down and I was kind of surprised I wasn't going down with them. It is weird trying to describe it, but usually, it's almost like you know when you're going to get tackled and when you're not going to get tackled. That play was a time when I had that surprised feeling. I thought, okay, I'm not down yet. I braced myself, and then I remember being able to break free and run to the goal.

Former Bears linebacker Brian Cox said I once made him miss four tackles in a single play—a great tribute from a great player. Former Packers and Eagles defensive end Reggie White said I was the only player he ever feared physically. "There was one guy since I've been playing that I was afraid of, because he could beat us at any moment. That was Barry." I admired Reggie both as a player and as a person, so this respect for my running skills meant a lot to me.

I played against some great defenders and some great defensive coaches, including former linebacker Lawrence Taylor of the New York Giants, as well as Tony Dungy, when he was the defensive coordinator for the Minnesota Vikings and later the head coach for the Tampa Bay Buccaneers.

These players and coaches—more on them in the next chapters—slowed me down, and sometimes, they stopped me. I'll have to ask them how they did it. Taylor once told me after a game he was relieved to see we weren't running out of an I-formation. If we had used that formation, he said, they wouldn't have been able to stop me. I remember thinking, "Wow. What a compliment."

Looking back on my career, I'm grateful for God's gift to me. I loved to run, and I feel blessed that I was able to spend many years doing it. When a vision becomes a reality, it's a great feeling.

WORDS FROM LOUIS OLIVER FORMER MIAMI DOLPHINS SAFETY

Barry and I were roommates with the Playboy All-American team in 1988, and we got to know each other, but I only got a chance to play against him once. The game was in Detroit, in 1991. As we prepared for the Lions, our plan was to get as many guys around Barry Sanders as possible and try to get a good tackle on him. That was tough to do. You rarely saw anybody really get a shot on him, helmet to helmet.

When you're trying to stop him, you surround him, you try to contain him. You're also trying not to make the ESPN highlights with him faking you out of your shoes. I remember on one play, they threw a flare pass to the side of the field, and I came running up on him.

I got about five yards away and just stopped, waiting to see what he was going to do. I wasn't about to let him make me look like a fool. I wasn't going to make "Sports Center" that night, with Chris Berman making funny remarks about me. When you're trying to tackle Barry Sanders, there's a very high probability that this will happen to you.

At the end of the game, I was relieved to be done with it. We lost 17-13, but I'd made 13 tackles and didn't get made to look stupid by Barry. We did a pretty good job of keeping him surrounded, but he still hit us for over a hundred yards.

As far as guys who were tough to tackle, I'd put him right at the top. A big back might be tough to bring down, but you can get a hit on him. He'll let you make contact. But tackling Barry was like tackling a slippery eel in the ocean.

CHAPTER ELEVEN

Rivals

Something about the word "rivalry" bothers me. It seems to imply jealousy or dislike. It never was like that with me and the people I played against. Though we were rivals, I guess, in the traditional sense of the word, I didn't see them as enemies or feel negative emotions toward them. And I had a unique perspective, because every defender on the other team was keying on me.

During one game, when word got out that I had a sore ankle, I can remember guys in the post-play scrum trying to twist my ankle. If the turf under the piles of players on top of me could talk, it could tell you things that wouldn't get past a censor. You certainly couldn't print what was said. One of the more tame comments was something like, "Not today! Not today!" By that phrase, they meant I wouldn't be making any spectacular runs against their defense that day. I never said anything back. I'd smile, nod and trot back to the huddle, and then I'd come flying back hard on the next play. If I accomplished my goal, I really didn't need to say anything, did I?

But I didn't dislike anyone. I have to admit, I enjoyed the trash talk. It made the games more fun, more challenging. The talk often brought out the best in me, and I knew it was never personal. When the game ended, that type of talk stopped.

One "rival" running back who I like a lot is Emmitt Smith, who is now retired. He's always been very complimentary to me and is just a genuine, authentic person. Though we played in the league together for years, I didn't realize until later that he was such a fun-loving guy around his teammates. He's a lot more outgoing than I thought. When he asked me to join his Run for the Record campaign in 2002, I was excited to be part of it. Though Emmitt is a great guy, we did compete. Before one of the Pro Bowls, for example, the two of us disappeared for a friendly competition—nothing serious, just fun-and-games type of stuff. We were throwing the ball with either hand, running and juking, stuff like that. We were trying to out-do each other, but I can't say if we declared a winner. Since he still holds the career rushing record, with 18,355 yards, breaking the previous record held by Walter Payton in 2002, I'll say that he won.

Neal Anderson was another back I really admired. At the beginning of my career, whenever I'd go into a contract negotiation, I would always hear some reference to, "Neal Anderson-type money." Whenever we played the Bears, there was always a little bit of competition among the backs—who could pull off the best runs, who could gain the most yards, things like that. Anderson was a great rival in that way. I've always felt he was a very underrated player. He made plenty of long, spectacular runs, and he had game-breaking speed that a lot of fans don't always associate with him. People didn't know he was so fast.

> I enjoyed those types of rivalries, and I enjoyed them even more on certain fields. Games took on a special significance, because of the stadium's place in football lore, and because of the current players still carrying the team's banner of excellence.

Playing at Green Bay against Brett Favre was a treat in that way. Favre was a great player who brought an extra bit of energy to the game. Playing against Troy Aikman, Joe Montana and Steve Young were special moments, too. I recognized we were competing, but I couldn't help but be a fan and witness with the rest of the crowd just why these men were so special. It was great being on the same field with them.

TOUGH DEFENDERS

I could only compare numbers with my fellow running backs in the league, but I had to go head-to-head against my defensive rivals. John Lynch, former safety for the Tampa Bay Buccaneers, was one of those guys. I wanted him accounted for on blocking assignments. I always wanted to know where he was. The same is true for Brian Cox, formerly of the Chicago Bears. He was going to take his shot no matter what. He'd say, "Forget what I've been practicing all week. I'm going to take my shot and whatever happens, happens."

John and Brian weren't the only ones. There were other players, too, who might be called rivals—guys I wanted to avoid. But if I had a rivalry with a defensive unit, it had to be the Minnesota Vikings. Whenever we played the Vikings, there was always some competition. They had great hitters, such as Joey Browner. He would have made a good Raiders player. Back in the early '90s, they had a great defense—one of those unique defenses that don't come around often. They had Browner, Chris Doleman, Keith Millard and Henry Thomas. How do you get all those guys on the same team?

And they had a genius for a defensive coordinator—Tony Dungy, who later became the head coach for the Indianapolis Colts. I faced Tony with the Vikings, then later with Tampa Bay. Tony always had his teams ready to play, especially the defense. I looked forward to the challenges he'd lay out for us. I'm sure the other teams studied what Dungy and those guys were doing to bottle me up, but not everyone could do it. Other teams didn't have the personnel to do what the Vikings were doing. The success they had in stopping me is a testament to their defense.

Some of those other teams weren't above some creative preparation of their own. I saw a videotape in which one team's assistant coach said the staff actually brought a chicken to use in their scout offense to simulate my herky-jerky running style. I'm not sure it worked, though, because apparently they couldn't get the lazy chicken to run.

Another coach I admired a lot was Bill Parcells, who I faced several times, including when he coached the New York Jets. You could see at field level just how much he raised the level of play. You could tell his players were equipped with something extra. When you lined up against a Parcells team, you almost felt as if you were not only facing inspired players, but the coach as well, because his influence extended from sideline to sideline, and from end zone to end zone.

Though I mentioned some defensive players who I wanted to avoid on the field, let me also say some of those guys were the nicest people off the field. I especially liked, as well as admired, Reggie White and Mike Singletary. During the game, I was always conscious of them. We all played in the same division, so I lined up against them often, and they were truly the best I played against. After the game, Mike would always come up to me and tell me to take care of myself, to be careful, almost like a big brother. He seemed genuinely concerned.

I spent more time off the field with Reggie. I don't want to say he was a gentle giant, but he was a very pleasant and good person. He wanted the best for me off the field and tried to steer me around the pitfalls of making bad choices where friends were concerned. He took an interest in my personal life and made sure I had good people around me. He just reached out as a friend. It was always so interesting to see a guy who manhandled 300-pound linemen, but who also had such a gentle spirit. On the field, you'd better be ready to compete against Reggie. Off the field, it's hard to imagine feeling like he was a rival.

WORDS FROM EMMITT SMITH
NFL CAREER LEADING RUSHER

I guess you could say Barry and I were rivals in that we were always very conscious of each other. When I'd watch ESPN after a game, I always wanted to see what B. Sanders had done that day. For me, it was one of those things where I had to know what he was doing. And I knew if anybody had a chance to have a breakout game any week, it was Barry.

When I first met him, I was in awe, because I'd seen him run- in college and saw what he could do, and then I saw what he could do in the NFL. I thought, this guy here's the best. I knew if he was the best, I would have to do everything in my power to achieve his level and pass it, if I was going to make myself the best.

Barry Sanders, shown left, is standing with Emmitt Smith during the NFL Top 100 Greatest Players, an anual television series that counts down the top 100 players int he NFL, chosen by other players. The series is on the NFL Network.

His ability to stop, restart and change direction, all within a five-yard radius, is better than anybody I ever saw. His hips were amazing. It looked like he almost could turn them completely around his back. And he had great balance, great leg strength and great speed. He was fast. Some people underestimate his speed, saying he was more quick than fast.

I can't think of any runner who compares to him. People often bring up Gale Sayers, but I've watched Sayers, and he didn't do any of the things you saw Barry do. Sayers had speed and agility, no question, but he never did the things Barry did every time you watched him. I've never seen anybody who has the abilities Barry possessed.

One of those abilities, and one you don't hear a lot of people talk about, was his ability to avoid the big hit. Guys couldn't get a good hit on him, which was important, because that kept him healthy and in the game. Some people criticized him, saying he was flashy, but too many times, he'd lose two or three yards, because of his running style. But he never had an All-Pro offensive line in front of him, opening up holes. He lost yards sometimes, because he was too busy trying to make five guys miss.

At the same time, I don't get into those discussions about what he could have done if he had played on a better team. You just don't know. It might have helped him to have a better surrounding cast, but then you have to wonder if he would have gotten as many touches as he got. Maybe he would, and maybe he wouldn't. Everybody's got an opinion. I think it's better to focus on and remember what he did do, than get into all of that speculation.

As for being rivals, I'll say when the Cowboys played the Lions, I was intent on watching what he was doing, and I wanted to have a better day than he did. I would appreciate his runs and admire what he was doing, but as an individual, when you're playing against one of the best, you want to dominate, so you can show you're one of the best, too.

But the only time I ever would root against him was when we were playing against him. Barry is a prince of a guy. He's quiet and very reserved, at least until you get to know him. He's an all-around good person, and so when we weren't playing against him, I was rooting for him to do well. I was with him.

WORDS FROM MIKE SINGLETARY FORMER CHICAGO BEARS LINEBACKER

The biggest thing about playing against Barry was you knew it wasn't over until it was over. That rule applied to games as well as to individual plays. There was a play I remember, when we thought we had him—seven or eight guys right there on him, and the next thing I knew, he was running down the field for a touchdown.

I've never seen anyone, or played against anyone, who was like him. He defied all the rules of tackling. Even if you did everything you're supposed to do—got your feet right, looked at his belly button, positioned yourself, wrapped him up—he still would run past you. He had great vision and great feet. And he had the ability to always move those feet, even when you had him wrapped up. If you didn't get his feet, you weren't going to get him.

To have success against him, you had to be a disciplined defense, and you had to have perfect technique. You couldn't just lunge at him. If you were able to get him running east to west, you had a chance. If he was moving north to south, forget about it. He was going to get you.

I guess I played against him maybe eight times. The first time we played against him was his rookie year. We had heard about him and watched some film of him, and we said, "This kid has been making other teams look silly. Let's show him how the Bears play defense." Then he gained something like 120 yards against us. We couldn't believe it. Nobody did that to the Bears. After that first game, I knew the kid was special. It wasn't just a matter of being a good back or having a good game. This kid was special.

The Lions were in our division, so we saw a lot of him. If he wasn't going to play for some reason, we were more at ease against them. In a lot of ways, Barry was that team, and I say that with no disrespect to the other guys. They'll understand what I'm saying. When he was there, they played differently. They walked onto the field differently. The coaches coached differently.

Even if he beat you or made you look bad, you couldn't get mad at him. He was such a class kid, such a gentleman. When he scored, he didn't slam the ball down. He didn't tell guys he had made them look bad. And he could have done that, because he sure had plenty of chances to do it. But Barry was a quality person with a lot of character, and he didn't feel the need to prove anything to anybody or show-up anybody. He would just go about his business. That was Barry.

CHAPTER TWELVE

Coaches

One of my first coaches was one of my favorites, a man named William McNeal. He was my eighth-grade coach for the Wichita Colts, a Little League team. He helped me believe in myself with his encouraging attitude.

He didn't play favorites, and he paid as much attention to the weakest players as he did to the strongest. It wasn't one of those situations where if you weren't as big or as fast as other kids on the team he'd forget about you. His confidence in us made us all better players. He was great with kids. He was jovial and just out there to have a good time.

I had a different experience with another of my coaches, as I mentioned earlier. My ninth-grade year was really the first one I can remember not being a factor on the team.

I wasn't a factor at all. I hardly ever played. As I said before, the coach and Daddy got into it about that, too. Daddy was disappointed about my lack of playing time.

In a previous chapter, I mentioned Dale Burkholder, my coach during my senior year in high school. He may have been one of the most influential people in my life, outside my family. He might be my favorite coach in all the years I played. Coach B, who later was an assistant principal in Topeka, was the type of coach I'd want for my son. He enjoyed his job as much as any coach I'd ever seen. He loved being around kids. We weren't a burden. He wasn't playing games with our heads, or telling us he was going to do one thing and then do something else. We trusted him.

If he disliked anyone, he didn't show it. It was fun for everyone. Everyone liked Coach B. I've heard stories about how he put his job on the line when he finally started me at tailback, over the objections of the athletic director, Bob Shepler, who as I discussed earlier, was the previous head coach. I don't have much to say about him. I'm not certain why he made the decisions he made.

> Beyond our high school friendship, Coach B really lobbied for me as a player to college recruiters and pestered the local media with my highlight tape to spread the word about me.

These were things I could never do for myself. I might never have made it to Oklahoma State to play for Pat Jones, if not for Coach B's help and lobbying.

Pat treated me fairly. He was a no-nonsense coach who brought the most out of his players. He was a good motivator. During my years at OSU, I learned a lot from him. Most of all, he taught me the academic side of football, the mental preparation and the study the players have to do before a game. I learned how to analyze defenses, looking for patterns and tendencies, while watching film of the upcoming opponent. By the time I declared for the draft, I was ready to play in the NFL. Pat had prepared me to be a good pro during my years playing for him.

COACHES IN THE NFL

After playing for Pat Jones, Wayne Fontes marked another change in direction. He had been the interim coach in 1988, taking over the team after the previous head coach, Darryl Rogers, was fired. My first year in the league was his first full year as a head coach. At the beginning, he probably listened to too many people and too many different ideas.

Considering how the Lions sort of plugged him in as a stop-gap, many of us wondered in that first year how much faith and confidence the organization actually had in him. Despite that situation, I think he developed into a good coach. The guys liked him. I always liked him. We always understood football was a business and we were in the business of winning games, but he also understood there was a time for fun, too. He liked to laugh, and he loved to have a good time. He wasn't so serious he couldn't laugh with players, or even at himself. He also tried to put his players first. He realized he needed the players as much as the players needed him.

With Wayne, players liked being there—in the locker room and on the field. When he was fired after the '96 season, after we finished 5-11, I was disappointed. I thought he deserved another chance. We'd been to the playoffs almost every other year with Wayne as our coach. We'd gotten close to a Super Bowl appearance with him.

When the Lions fired Wayne, they hired Bobby Ross, a hard-working, hard-charging coach who was a solid leader. He was demanding and extremely well organized. Our training schedules were so painstakingly arranged, we knew what we were going to do, almost by the minute. Many players believed management had brought in Coach Ross to shape up the team, perhaps blaming Wayne's final losing season on his personable style. Wayne was seen as a player's coach, and the Lions wanted a new approach.

Barry Sanders is shown with his former wife, Lauren Sanders, and former head coach of the Detroit Lions, Wayne Fontes.

Coach Ross put in long hours. He would arrive around five in the morning and work until 10 or 11 at night. Because I had played for him for only two years, I didn't get to know him well. I did think, however, he made some poor personnel decisions, though it's impossible to know if the decisions were made by him or by Chuck Schmidt.

He had a few quirks, too. For example, he didn't like guys on our team helping up guys on the other team. I didn't understand that attitude, which struck me as old-fashioned. What difference does it make to show a little sportsmanship? But he knew a lot about the game, and he demanded and deserved respect. From a personal stand-point, I benefited from his emphasis on the running game. Coach Ross gave me the ball, and that philosophy allowed me to gain over 2,000 yards in a season.

WORDS FROM WAYNE FONTES FORMER HEAD COACH OF THE DETROIT LIONS

When I was coaching Barry, players said I treated him a little special. I remember one year, at training camp, a veteran receiver stood up and told the rookies, "Coach has probably told you he treats everybody the same. Well, you see that little guy wearing number 20? Coach treats him differently. Don't you ever knock him down."

Everybody had a good laugh, but the player was right. I even had a no-contact rule in practice for Barry. Usually, that rule was only for the quarterbacks. The defensive guys like Jerry Ball and Chris Spielman would joke around and say they were going to rush in and crush Barry, but when the play was run, a hole would open up a mile wide.

That's how much they respected him. Every player on that team loved him. They knew he didn't need to prove anything in practice. When the game started, Barry would be ready.

He would make sure he was ready. After a long practice, when the players headed for the locker room, Barry would go down to the end of the field by himself and run sprints. Sometimes, he was still at it when the other guys had showered, gotten dressed and were headed home. They'd stop and watch him. He was amazing, and they knew it. In practice and on the field, he was a no-nonsense player. Everything was a hundred percent.

He was a great runner, because he was so well prepared, but he also had great instincts. He had a vision on the field few people have—knowing when a hole was opening up, seeing something downfield nobody else saw. It's like he had a sixth sense.

Before games, the players would do different things—listen to music or pound their pads against the wall. Spielman would always walk around in the shower. Barry would lie down with a towel over his head. I'd go around to each of them and shake hands, and when I came to Barry, he'd lift his hand without taking the towel away. He always could sense I was there.

Wayne Fontes
Detroit Lions Records

	Regular Season		Playoffs	
Year	W	L	W	L
1988	2	3	0	0
1989	7	9	0	0
1990	6	10	0	0
1991	12	4	1	1
1992	5	11	0	0
1993	10	6	0	1
1994	9	7	0	0
1995	10	6	0	0
1996	5	11	0	0
Totals	66	67	1	2

He was also one of the nicest people I've ever come across in coaching. As great a runner as he was, he was an even better person. He was an unselfish guy. He didn't care if he touched the ball four times or 20, if the team was winning, and he always acknowledged the blocking of his teammates. If you had a daughter, you'd say this is the perfect guy for her. I remember liking him the first time I met him, and that feeling never changed. I treated him differently, because he was special. He made my eight years in Detroit very memorable.

CHAPTER THIRTEEN

2,053

With so many regular-season games, the 1,000-yard season for a running back isn't the standard of success it used to be when a season was only 12 or 14 games long. Average 62.5 yards over 16 weeks, and you're there.

In 1998, with two games left in the season, 13 players already had gained 1,000 yards, and six others were poised to reach the mark. At the time, there'd never been 16 players with 1,000-yard seasons. It seems to me that 1,200 or 1,400 yards is more of a standard. In 1985, nine players had 1,200 or more yards: Marcus Allen, Gerald Riggs, Walter Payton, Joe Morris, Freeman McNeil, Tony Dorsett, James Wilder, Eric Dickerson and Craig James.

I was fortunate enough during my career to average nearly 1,500 yards a season, but until I had a season in which I got close to 2,000 yards, I didn't think that milestone was possible for me. In 1994, I was 17 yards shy of 1,900. At the time, only two running backs had passed the 2,000-yard threshold: Dickerson, with 2,105, in 1984; and O.J. Simpson, with 2,003, in 1973.

At the beginning of 1997, the season I finally cracked the 2,000-yard mark, it didn't appear as if I'd be joining them. I felt good. I felt strong. But after two games, I had only 53 yards, and reporters started reminding me that I was 29. In other words, I was getting old.

But I felt like 2,000 was a possibility. I'd run for 1,800 before. I knew that reaching 2,000 depended, to some extent, on what was going on with the team, but I felt if I stayed healthy and in the right situation, it was possible. In those first games, against Atlanta and Tampa Bay, I didn't get a lot of carries. Also, in the game against the Buccaneers, I had 102 receiving yards and even scored a touchdown, so I felt like I was producing. I didn't

Barry Sanders being hoisted on the shoulders of teammates in December 1997, after gaining 2,053 yards for the season.

feel old. I was ready and able to have a good year. I made myself the player I was, because I always wanted to see what I could do next. I wanted to see if I could reach the next level.

Putting my own feelings and goals aside, I had guys blocking for me who really wanted me to get the milestone. I pushed for it as much for them as for myself. After those first two games in '97, however, the goal might have seemed to be a little out of reach. Then things changed. The yards piled up so quickly, my success surprised even me. It had been an up-and-down season for the team, but I was having my best year in years. One game, at Tampa Bay, I had two runs longer than 80 yards, and finished with 215 yards on the day.

I can't say that I expected to do it. In the game of pro football, you just never know. Everything has to line up right for you to be able to accomplish something like that. That day in Tampa—Oct. 12—was just such a day, despite the warm Florida weather. Coming there from Detroit, we were thinking about a whole other set of problems, such as cramping up, losing water, fading out, because of the heat.

After the first long run, I remember thinking, "Okay, you got the 80-yard run, and the D is going to be pretty tight the rest of the game." And so when the second one came, I was shocked. In fact, while I was running, I was assuming either I was going to get tired, burn out and somebody was going to catch me, or I wasn't going to make it.

REACHING 2,000

We rode the momentum of the win at Tampa Bay all the way until the last game of the season. Going into that game at home against the New York Jets, I needed more than 130 yards to reach 2,000 yards, and the team needed this win to earn a play-off berth. The pressure was intense, but I found myself enjoying it, energized by the challenge. I felt renewed.

Reaching 2,000 was probably the first individual performance record I really, really wanted. The Heisman, though—I enjoyed the honor of receiving it, just didn't seem real. At the time, I didn't see myself as being in the same league with others who'd won the award. From high school to the pros, as I mentioned earlier, I was content to sit out of the end of games that my team had won, even when I was just a few yards short of rushing titles. Building up yardage against a beaten opponent, for your own personal gain, just never seemed respectful or dignified to me.

This time, however, was different. I wanted that 2,000. As we prepared to play the Jets, the whole country seemed to be watching to see if I could get it. I had 20 to 30 family members and friends watching the game from my home, and a dozen more in the stands.

The game tested our resolve and the crowd's nerves. We fell behind a Jets team that had a pretty good scheme for stopping us. I'd read that a few years before the game, Coach Bill

Parcells had stolen a Super Bowl for his team at the time, the New York Giants, by shortening the game against the offensively superior Buffalo Bills. On this day, in the Silverdome, he seemed to be doing the same thing. He ran short plays that ate up the clock, and kept the ball out of our offense's hands and out of my hands, too.

His strategy worked for a while. The Jets scored 10 points in the first 12 minutes. At that stage of the game, I only had eight carries and 20 yards. The crowd and my teammates were getting antsy. It wasn't until the third quarter that I really became a factor. On third and three, from our 36 yard line, Scott Mitchell handed me the ball, and I sliced through the line for a 47-yard run.

On the next play, I shot off our left tackle and was in the end zone 15 yards later. We took the lead and never looked back. That 15-yard run turned out to be the winning touchdown. I finished the game with 184 yards, and I finished the season with 2,053. I ended the 1997 season with a 6.1 yards per carry average, which was the third best season average among players with at least 200 attempts, behind Jim Brown in 1963 with 6.4 yards per carry and Jamaal Charles in 2010 with 6.4 yards per carry.

Interestingly, after the game, Daddy whispered to my friend, Mark, that I was as good, if not better, than Jim Brown at the time. Daddy had always made a big deal saying Jim Brown wasn't just better than me, he was a man among boys. But Daddy, of all people, told Mark that he didn't want to sound vain, bragging on his own son. He's never told me he thought I was better. He just told Mark, as far as I know.

DOUBTS ABOUT THE FUTURE

I was proud of my accomplishment, but it was tempered by yet another blow. One of my teammates, Reggie Brown, suffered a serious spinal cord injury during the game with the Jets. He had to be given mouth-to-mouth resuscitation on the field. The experience left me thinking more than ever about my professional mortality. As I mentioned in an earlier chapter, my teammate, Mike Utley, had suffered a similar injury in 1991, and now Reggie was down.

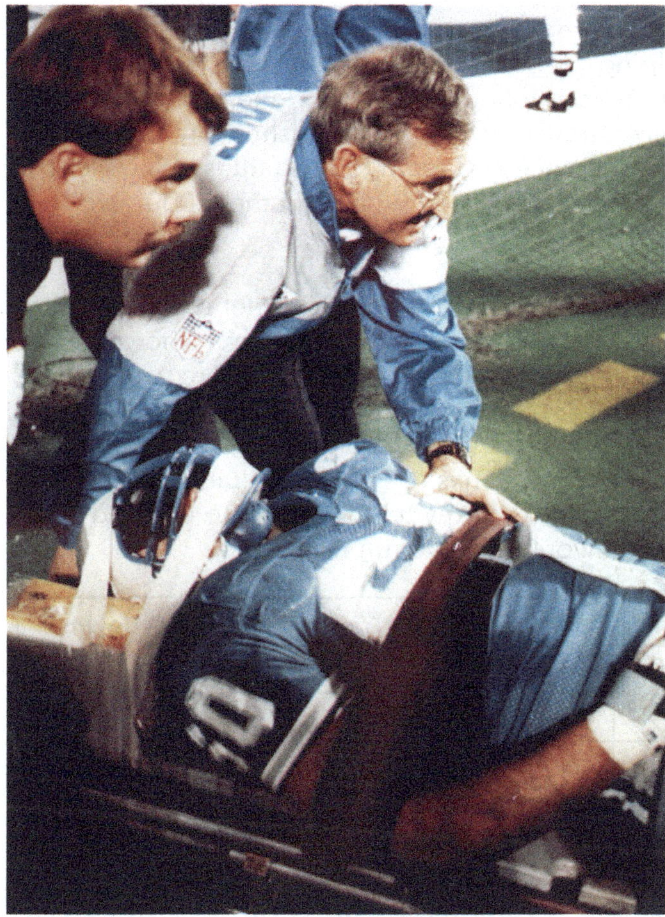

Former Detroit Lions player Reggie Brown is being put on a stretcher during a game.

What happened to them truly frightened me. In the back of every player's mind, there is an awareness of the barbaric, dangerous nature of the game.

But then, to have that sort of subtle awareness shattered by an event right in front of you sobers you. To see the tragedy and know these people and like them, and see how it affects their lives, and to be on the field when it happens ... I don't know. That's almost enough to make you want to quit right there.

That's enough to make you say, how do you go on?

When someone is injured, it lingers. It's always on your mind. It is so eerie. You understand that not only can you get seriously injured, but you can actually die.

I had considered walking away before the season, and Reggie's injury wasn't helping me to stay committed to the game. When I stopped to take an accounting of what I'd done to that point in my career, I realized how much I'd accomplished already. I had gained league, conference and team rushing titles; a highlight reel full of electrifying runs; a membership in the 2,000-yard club; and an MVP.

Reaching that milestone was something to remember. In the history of the NFL, and despite all the great backs who played before me, I was the third player with 2,000 or more yards in a season, behind O.J. Simpson in 1973 and Eric Dickerson in 1984. Only five other players have accomplished this feat since I retired. Of course, I give thanks to God for helping me achieve that goal. I also give thanks to my teammates who blocked for me. Without them, I wouldn't have run far at all.

Week/Opponent	***Rushes***	***Yards***	***Touchdowns***
1. Atlanta	15	33	0
2. Tampa Bay	10	20	1
3. Chicago	19	161	0
4. New Orleans	18	133	1
5. Green Bay	28	139	0
6. Buffalo	25	107	0
7. Tampa Bay	24	215	3
8. New York Giants	24	105	1
9. Green Bay	23	105	0
10. Washington	15	105	1
11. Minnesota	19	108	0
12. Indianapolis	24	216	2
13. Chicago	19	167	3
14. Miami	30	137	1
15. Minnesota	19	138	0
16. New York Jets	23	184	1
TOTALS	***335***	***2,053***	***14***

In reaching 2,000, I set another record of 14 consecutive 100-yard games. No one had ever done that before, and that record means as much to me as any other. Considering the level of competition in the game, I'll always be especially proud of that particular record.

That season gave me pride for a number of reasons. Winning the Most Valuable Player award was a great honor, and by gaining 2,053 yards, I jumped from seventh to second on the all-time rushing list at that time. During the year, I passed Marcus Allen, Franco Harris, Jim Brown, Tony Dorsett and Eric Dickerson. Now I am fourth on the all-time rushing list behind Emmitt Smith, Walter Payton and Frank Gore.

As I've said, numbers don't mean all that much to me, but being in the company of those great players, especially Jim Brown, meant a great deal to me. Chasing Walter Payton's record, however, never seemed nearly as important to me as it did to a lot of the fans and to the sports media. I had already achieved a level of success that gave me much satisfaction and pride. I didn't need to pass Walter to prove anything to myself.

A goal that I still hadn't realized, however, was playing in the Super Bowl, and all of the statical achievements didn't put the team any closer to playing in the big game. The win against the Jets did put us in the playoffs and sent us back to Tampa Bay to play in the Wild-Card game.

But unlike the day earlier in the season, when I made the two 80-yard runs, this time we lost. There were no 80-yard runs for me. Instead, I finished with 65 yards on 18 carries, and the Bucs beat us 20-10. It was another frustrating end of a season. Though I remained proud of the records, and despite everything I'd been able to accomplish, I was increasingly unsure about my professional future.

WORDS FROM KEVIN GLOVER FORMER TEAMMATE, DETROIT LIONS

Barry was never into records and titles, but the year he gained over 2,000 yards was special. We knew he'd be near the top of the league, like he always was, but nobody thought he'd get to 2,000, especially after the first two games, when he had only 53 yards. We were still learning a new offensive system, so the slow start wasn't his fault. And when you look at it, he gained 2,000 yards in 14 games.

As the season went on and he kept getting 100-yard games, the linemen knew he had a chance at 2,000, but we never discussed it with him. The linemen always went out on Thursday night, and with three games left in the season, we sat together and figured out what he would have to average to get 2,000. We decided to try to help him get what he needed. We had so much respect for him.

You knew, on any given play, he could go all the way, and that made you give a little extra. I remember one play during that year, in a game against Green Bay. It was third and 18, and the coach called a counter-play—a run. In the huddle we were thinking, "Why aren't we passing?" We could have doubted the play call and not given a full effort, but with Barry in the game, there was always a chance. So we gave it everything, and Barry broke off a big run and scored a touchdown.

For personal reasons, I'll always remember the last run. He'd gotten the 2,000 yards late in the game on a short run, maybe two yards. Then, near the end of the game, he broke off a 53-yarder. I told him thanks for going out of bounds when he did, because he ended up with 2,053 for the year. His number was 20 and mine was 53, and that was the last game we'd ever play together as teammates. I'll never forget it.

CHAPTER FOURTEEN

Run From the Record

Soon after I reached the 2,000-season mark, the talk around me moved to a new mountain: Walter Payton's career rushing record of 16,726 yards. By the end of the 1998 season, I was only 1,457 yards behind Walter, and I'd been averaging more than 1,500 yards a season, so me setting a new record looked like a sure thing.

People took notice, and I quickly found myself in the middle of "Run for the Record," a licensing and sponsorship campaign put together by Access Group of Miami, sports-and-entertainment marketing company.

They planned to recruit sponsors to leverage my march to the record to sell cars, cereal, sportswear and other products. The idea interested me, in part because of the charity affiliations involved with it: The Boys and Girls Club of South Central Kansas, The Scleroderma Research Foundation and the Detroit Lions Foundation.

The proposal was exciting, in some ways, but it also thrust me into the middle of a marketing frenzy, which made me uneasy.

The "Run for the Record" campaign was strange from the start. As I discussed in an earlier chapter, I've never been fond of public attention or a lot of dealing with the media. I don't mean to sound aloof; being in the spotlight just isn't in my nature.

Not long after the campaign began, I found myself skipping rallies and functions meant to drum up support, spark interest with fans and attract sponsors. To make matters more complicated, Bobby Ross hated the idea, saying the campaign would weaken team chemistry by focusing on one player instead of the team. As I said earlier, Bobby was a traditionalist, but he did have a point. I didn't want the focus of the team to be on me. The focus should be on doing whatever it takes to win games.

I wondered if that focus was possible, amid all the media and marketing hoopla. Meanwhile, my frustrations with management continued to mount, while my love for the game spilled out of me.

I felt terrible and I am sure it felt like I was springing this on my agents, but I had been thinking about retiring for a while, so to me it did not feel as shocking. I retired three days after Wheaties put a cereal box out saying "Fueling Barry's Run for the Record." Many companies had their ads ready to go for the 1999 season.

I made sure that all the contracts had an "out" clause —a clause that allowed for my retirement. They all must have assumed no one would retire so close to one of the most sacred records in professional sports. Who would pass on millions of dollars in endorsements? Who would walk out over $30-million in deals that did not risk me getting hit?

I never played for money or records, I played because I loved football and that love was pretty much gone.

I am proud to say that I still work with Nike and many brands that were with me back in 1998.

CHAPTER FIFTEEN

I Knew it was Over

I talked about retiring, long before doing it. Most of the time, jokingly. One time, while stretching with Herman Moore and Tracey Scroggins, I teased that one day, while they were all stretching, I'd suddenly walk into the locker room and never come back. They thought the idea was hilarious.

But when the end finally came, it wasn't at all funny. I cried, and I'm not certain why. Maybe the tears came pouring out, because I had just endured perhaps the most emotionally draining season I'd ever played—a 5-11 season, our second in the past three. We had made the playoffs the previous year, and everyone had expected us to do better.

Maybe I cried, because I knew, for the first time since I could remember, I wouldn't be playing football anymore. An all-consuming part of my life had just died.

It felt like losing a close friend, a fulfilling relationship or a sustaining hopefulness. Or all three. The tears could have come from exhaustion, the kind of fatigue a marathoner's mind fights off, long after his or her body is supposed to have shut down from exertion.

In my last game, we were playing in Baltimore against the Ravens on a raw, rainy afternoon in December of 1998. During my career, I rarely fumbled, but I had uncharacteristically let the ball—and the game—slip through my fingers. We lost 19-10.

Also uncharacteristically, the guy who never exploded in celebration when crossing the goal line, the guy who kept his emotions tucked away as tightly as he tucked away the football, cried in

FREEP.COM | SUNDAY, JULY 21, 2019 | 9C

Cover story Gone, Barry, Gone

BARRY'S GREAT ESCAPE

Barry Sanders arrives alone at London's Gatwick Airport from Detroit on July 28, 1999, the same day he announced his retirement from the NFL. Sanders was only 1,458 yards shy of breaking the NFL career rushing record at the time of his retirement. ALASTAIR GRANT/ASSOCIATED PRESS

Sanders made the most bizarre dash of his career hours after retirement and headed overseas

Gene Myers
Special to Detroit Free Press
USA TODAY NETWORK

Gene Myers arrived at the Detroit Free Press from the University of Kansas in May 1983. He spent his last 22½ years as sports editor, retiring in late 2015. (The Lions had nine head coaches during his tenure.) Myers, 59, was in the Pontiac Silverdome stands when the Lions won their only playoff game since 1957 and when Barry Sanders reached 2,000 rushing yards the day Reggie Brown nearly died. Myers was in his downtown office the night Sanders retired on the eve of training camp in 1999.

Twenty years, eh? All I can do is laugh about those crazy few days and nights – for the Lions, for the fans, at the Free Press.

I immediately think of the photo of Sanders when he landed in London. Only the Lions could have one of the most iconic photos in team history be of their best player pulling his carry-on bags in a foreign airport when he should have been unpacking them in training camp.

I almost hate to admit it, but I was shocked when the Free Press was tipped off that Sanders was at Metro Airport, apparently waiting for an evening flight to London. If it were 2019 instead of 1999, without a doubt, somebody would have shot video of Sanders at the gate and it would have gone viral in minutes. But in 1999 all we had was an anonymous caller and no real proof of validity.

I was working late in the office that July night, but not because we feared Sanders was about to retire. Yeah, there were plenty of signs of tension – especially because his father kept lambasting the offense devised by Bobby Ross and Sylvester Croom. Maybe Sanders wouldn't report to camp right away in protest or to force a trade or to give his dad more airtime. But what athlete quits in his prime, gives up millions in guaranteed earnings and, as the topper, knows he must pay back $7 million from his signing bonus? Betcha even Jim Brown would have suited up again under those circumstances!

When Free Press copy editor Bill Collison heard about the Sanders tip, he had good reason not to dismiss it. His daughter, Maggie, was at Metro at that very moment, about to board a flight to Gatwick with her church choir. He couldn't reach her, of course, because in those days so few of us had cell phones, especially a young girl going overseas.

However, after Bill hustled in to see me, it didn't take long for Curt Sylvester, our Lions beat reporter, to reach David Ware, one of Sanders' two agents. Ware told Curt that Sanders had decided to retire and had told his agents that afternoon with a phone call and a written statement. The news was to be announced the next day. The Lions, caught off guard and befuddled, declined comment.

Ware also said Sanders was with his family in Wichita. To this day, I don't know whether Ware was lying about his whereabouts, whether Sanders didn't even tell his agents about his vacation plans or whether Sanders at the time didn't know where he would go other than not to training camp in Saginaw. The Free Press' 1A story reported that Ware said Sanders was in Kansas but that others placed him at Metro, possibly headed to London.

It was so late at night that we didn't have time for too much coverage in the next morning's paper. The big headline in the Sports section was "Bye, Barry" – with a story by Curt that Ron Rivers would get the ball and a column by the late Drew Sharp with the headline "Sanders quits on teammates, fans."

The next day was a ton of fun, one of those days that reminds you why you got into journalism. The Free Press had six pages of Sanders coverage. His abrupt departure turned a huge news story – the opening of the MGM Grand, Detroit's first casino – into a water cooler afterthought. The real issue of the day: Should fans direct their anger at Sanders or the Lions.

I just checked out the pages from that day. The 1A photo showed a man eating his lunch with the giant Barry Sanders mural in the background. The Sports photo, of course, showed Sanders and his carry-ons at Gatwick with the headline "No turning back." Among the other headlines that day: "Sanders says he isn't in a London fog," "See Barry run: Exit's a fast one," "Lions are surprised, act prepared," "Who goofed? Ross, execs to blame, too," "Fans debate if Lions worth time, money," "Team has mixed emotions," "Dad: If Ross were gone, son wouldn't be," "Barry, you were great, but not the greatest," and "Few options for Barry's successor."

At the time, I think most fans were beyond irked with Sanders. They had grown accustomed to the Lions annually being a hot mess. But Barry was greatness personified. With an average Barry year, he would have become the NFL's all-time leading rusher. That meant a lot to the fans of a perennial afterthought franchise. Obviously, it didn't mean so much to Sanders. And that's so hard – still – for all us Average Joes and Janes to understand.

These days, though, I think most people blame the Lions. And why not? What credibility do you have with one playoff victory in 60-plus years? And when you also botched it with your superstars this century, Calvin Johnson and Ndamukong Suh?

As I said, I was shocked that night in July. But by the next morning I wasn't. I realized that with the Lions being the Lions and Sanders' "mysterious 'That's Barry' ways" – a phrase coined by the Free Press' Steve Schrader – the Lions-Sanders relationship ended in the only possible way: With something so bizarre that it would become legendary – equal parts ridiculous, unexplainable, expensive, comical and sad.

On the beat

Curt Sylvester, longtime Free Press sports writer, covered the Lions for 26 seasons before retiring in 2005. Here's what he recalled about the fateful day of Barry Sanders' retirement:

"Obviously it caught everybody by surprise. I remember the first thing that crossed my mind was how the hell am I going to get this story? How am I going to develop this because you couldn't get a hold of anybody on the phone. Barry, he was obviously not going to talk. ...

"In the back of your mind, separate from the story, you're thinking: What's going to happen to the Lions now? Because no disrespect to Ron Rivers, but he was a backup. He'd run a few plays if Barry got nicked or something in a game. But he wasn't a full-service running back. And you're thinking: Do they have the quarterback and the receivers to pick up the slack. I didn't really think that they did.

"It was a very unusual time. And then camp opened and you talked to players about it. And most players were supportive of Barry, at least publicly. But some guys it just bothered them that Barry waited until the last minute and really left them high and dry without an NFL-caliber running game. So they were a little bit miffed at that. ...

"The thing is, it didn't surprise me at all that this was the way Barry decided to go out. And it didn't surprise me at all that he did it at the last minute. He never sought the spotlight. He didn't like to be in the spotlight, even back then. He had adjusted. He had fun with the media and he could live with being in the spotlight.

"And my own feeling was that he certainly didn't do it intentionally to put the Lions in bad spot waiting until the last minute. I think he just procrastinated. He knew if he called a press conference to announce it, it would bring all sorts of questions and attention and that was the last thing that he craved or wanted to endure. So he just put it off until there was no more putting it off and then said that's it, gave his buddy (at the Wichita Eagle) the story and it wasn't his problem anymore."

Livin' in Barry strange times

The following excerpt was published in the Free Press on July 29, 1999, two days after Barry Sanders retired:

Things Barry Sanders might do in his retirement:

- Appear in a remake of "The Dirty Dozen."
- Move to Sweden.
- File for workers comp.
- Do all the things he's never had time for, like return Bobby Ross' phone calls.
- Run for the Senate in New York.
- Think of excuses to skip his Hall of Fame induction.
- Watch the Super Bowl on TV, just as he always has.
- Don't know. Ask his dad.

The legacy

Things we'll remember Barry for:

- All those long touchdown runs ... and the times No. 20 was caught from behind, short of the end zone.
- Skipping minicamps ... but showing up for games.
- His incredible, highlight-reel escapes from tacklers ... when he wasn't stopped behind the line of scrimmage.
- Coaches who didn't quite seem to know how to use him ... and his seeming reluctance to adapt to their systems (and catch a darn pass).
- Remembering in wonder his big-yardage seasons ... but wondering why he didn't produce more in the playoffs.
- Being grateful for all the times he was the lone bright spot on dismal Lions teams ... but resenting the way he's walking away from them on the eve of, yes, another season of frustration.
- Chuckling at mysterious "That's Barry" ways over the years ... but wondering now what the heck he's thinking, and if we've really seen the last of him.

The building

What happens to the 15-story painting of Sanders on the Cadillac Tower building? Our suggestions for new wording:

- Thanks.
- Thanks for nothing.
- 15,269 yards, one playoff victory.
- 5-11, 9-7, 5-11 ...
- Which way to Saginaw?

Winners & losers

Winner: Walter Payton, whose rushing record of 16,726 remains unchallenged.

Loser: Bobby Ross, who seems destined to repeat Monte Clark's famous words: "See you in the cemetery."

Winner: ABC, which had the foresight not to schedule the Lions for "Monday Night Football."

Loser: Christmas Day, because who can't get excited about Bubby Brister vs. Ron Rivers in a beer-free Silverdome?

Detroit Free Press

SANDERS WALKS; AN ERA ENDS

This page is from the Detroit Free Press 20th anniversary of Barry Sanders' retirement.

front of several teammates in the locker room. The game hadn't been important to either team. Neither was headed for the playoffs. I think a few people saw me crying, but no one said anything. I was crying, because I knew it was over.

SHOTS TO THE PSYCHE

I'd considered leaving for years, and for no single reason. Around the middle of my career, the game became something else, almost a burden in a lot of ways, and I stopped loving it. My achievements in 1997 came in spite of my waning desire.

Ever watch a boxing match? The fight is rarely decided on one punch. Most fights amount to violent chess matches, in which the fighters bank and deposit pain, save and spend their energy. Stingers attack from their toes, circling and circling, and flicking jabs into the opponent's face, until the accumulation of blows and the loss of stamina topples the other fighter. Sluggers forge ahead, chewing through leather, swallowing punches, just to land a few stabbing body shots that send waves of pain rippling over the opponent's body, the kind of shots that steal your wind and your will.

I think that's what happened to me. I lost my will. I just wasn't willing anymore, and the series of shots I'd taken in the previous seasons siphoned off my commitment. Those shots weren't physical. They weren't collisions during games. Few people actually got hard shots on me in my 10 years in the league. I was still in great shape. My ninth year was my best ever. I'm referring more to shots to my psyche. Disappointments. Losses. Betrayals even.

A number of these shots involved the loss of key players, who either were traded away or allowed to go to other teams. We lost Jerry Ball (I used to live on Jerry's wife's cooking), Lomas Brown, Chris Spielman, Bennie Blades and others. It was difficult to lose All-Pro players and respected teammates, particularly when the problem didn't seem to involve money. The team was signing free agents for more money, and the contract negotiations with these new players seemed to go smoothly. Meanwhile, players who had proven their value to the team were discarded or ignored. When I wanted to restructure my contract, for example,

I had to hold out just to get management to the table.

I had thought about leaving, even before signing the next-to-the-last contract. The communication gap widened by the week, between Lions' management and me, mostly with GM Chuck Schmidt. While I was negotiating a new contract, I received another shot when I was told, "Just because you're the best player on the team doesn't mean you have to be the highest paid."

The comment didn't make me angry, but it did make me think: "Is this team serious about winning?" When I arrived in 1989, we were rebuilding. During the next few years, little by little, attendance started climbing, my jerseys began selling out and electricity was returning to the Silverdome.

And despite holding virtually every Lions rushing record, I continued to push myself. As I mentioned in an earlier chapter, when I was a rookie, I'd eat a grocery sack full of Suzy Q's and candy before a game. By the end of my career, I was eating boiled vegetables and keeping myself fit year-round.

But by 1998, we were in an awful slide back into rebuilding. After all those years, I'd come full circle. It was tough to stay focused and motivated. Walter Payton was right when he said if you can't play the way the game was meant to be played, you shouldn't play at all. I knew deep down that my heart wasn't in it anymore. I'd thought about retiring before the 1997 season, when I rushed for over 2,000 yards. I was running on fumes then.

By urging me on toward Walter's career rushing record, everyone was missing an important point: If rushing titles never motivated me before—as evidenced by me pulling myself out of games in high school, college and in my rookie season—then why would such a record be motivation to continue playing now?

When I was growing up, sports were everything to me. If I wasn't playing sports, I was thinking about playing, and if I wasn't thinking about it, I was dreaming about it. Making it to the pros was the ultimate, and I felt like I had so much to prove from the start. Coming from a small school and being criticized for not playing bigger schools (as if I made the schedules), I wanted to prove I was good enough to play pro ball, if only to myself.

Given my success in the league, I'd proven I was good enough, and so that motivation was gone. In the final few years of my career, I only had the team's success to motivate me. I wanted to win. But by those final years, I began to wonder seriously about the motivations of some of the people in the front office. It was hard to guess their bottom line, but it certainly wasn't winning.

TEAMMATES AND WINNING

When they got rid of Kevin Glover, they convinced me their goal wasn't anywhere close to being about winning games. In 1997, the season before he was traded, we were riding on the team plane together. Kevin and I used to sit next to each other on the plane on our road trips. He leaned over, and said, "You know what? You see how Bennie (Blades) isn't here anymore? You see how Lomas (Brown) is not here anymore? Next year, I'm not going to be here, because management doesn't want me here anymore."

I laughed. I couldn't believe it. There was no way Kevin was not going to be with the team the next year. He'd made the Pro Bowl two years, and he would make it again. Though '97 was the year I ran for 2,000 yards, Kevin was the true leader of the team. It showed in everything he did—from the practice field, to the locker room, to the games. He was someone we couldn't replace. But Kevin insisted management would see to it he wasn't around, and sure enough, they made the move, shipping him off to Seattle.

> I didn't realize it at the time, but part of me left with him, just as part of me left with those other guys I mentioned. Football may be a violent game, but it's all about love.

You have to love the game, and part of that love comes from your teammates, the guys who share the same goal of winning, the guys who create the locker room chemistry.

That dedication to winning, to doing well as part of a team of guys, is what drove me to diet, run and lift weights during the off-season. I wanted to win—for myself and for the team. I loved the game enough to do what it takes in March and April to prepare myself to play through the following January.

During games, I put everything into it, and so the realization that some of the people you worked for weren't as committed to winning as you were, slammed me harder than any linebacker had ever hit in my entire career. That realization trivialized everything I did during the off-season to prepare myself. It trivialized everything I dreamed about from the time I was a kid in Wichita, juking imaginary defenders in my front yard on North Volutsia.

As long as you know you're headed in the right direction, that you have a fighting chance at winning, all the effort makes sense and has meaning. But by 1997, it wasn't exactly clear what they were doing, other than shipping off proven players, and replacing them with young players who were unproven.

Losing was difficult, but this really wasn't about losing. Professional football is very competitive, and you're going to lose some games. Rather, it was more about not even trying to win, and I couldn't live with that. Playing in an NFL game, at my position especially, is like surviving a major car wreck. Multiply that feeling by 16 weeks, and you're lucky to walk away after the season. I was risking my neck, and I had two of my teammates go down with spinal cord injuries, for some bean-counter who really isn't committed to winning.

As time ran out in that game against the Ravens, it also ran out in my career. I decided they could go on without me. That game, even that season, was the knockout blow, the shot that took me from inevitability to completion.

TIME TO MOVE ON

The season had seemed to end before it even began. We lost our first three games and seven of our first nine. After winning three in a row, we lost to San Francisco and Jacksonville back-to-back to end any outside shot at the playoffs. It was difficult to even say we were playing for pride, when we'd been out of the running for so long and were missing a half-dozen injured starters.

Detroit Free Press | SUNDAY, JULY 21, 2019 | 1C

USA TODAY SPORTS

Great expectations? **Shawn Windsor:** Jim Harbaugh steers into hype at media days, but can he beat Ohio State? **Page 3C**

Sports

Barry Sanders stunningly retired on July 27, 1999, on the eve of Detroit Lions training camp. JULIAN H. GONZALEZ/DETROIT FREE PRESS

Gone, Barry, gone

Lions legend has few regrets 20 years after retiring on eve of training camp

Carlos Monarrez
Detroit Free Press
USA TODAY NETWORK

Twenty years is a long time. ‖ On a recent sweltering afternoon in late June, legendary Lions running back Barry Sanders stood underneath the boughs of the mighty oaks that form a canopy of shade in front of Detroit Golf Club. To those 100-foot-tall trees, 20 years is but a slice of time. To the golf club that was founded in 1899, 20 years is but a fraction. ‖ But in athletics, and especially in the NFL, 20 years is an eternity. ‖ Sanders had just finished a six-hour round of golf in the pro-am of the PGA Tour's inaugural Rocket Mortgage Classic. Yet he seemed fresh and unbothered by the heat in his white polo shirt and crisp navy trousers. He signed autographs for caddies and playing partners as fans nearby pressed up against a white-picket fence and held out souvenirs they hoped Sanders would sign. ‖ "Barry!" they called to him. "Barry!"

See BARRY, Page 11C

"... Yeah, the retirement part was a little clumsy. But the person that I was, I probably wouldn't (change anything)."

Barry Sanders Former Lions running back

One Tiger's mom against cancer: 'Just keep fighting'

Hicks' mother has battled disease for 4½ years

Jeff Seidel
Columnist
Detroit Free Press
USA TODAY NETWORK

Leslie Hicks wiped tears from her eyes, trying to hold a cell phone steady, but it was nearly impossible because all the emotion – the fear and pride and pain and happiness.

She wiped her eyes again.

Her husband, Tigers catcher John Hicks, crouched behind home plate, and his mother, Karen, was on the mound in Comerica Park, waiting to throw out a ceremonial pitch on Friday night before the Tigers' Pink Out the Park Game, an annual event that raises awareness about breast cancer and money to fight it.

Karen has been battling breast cancer for 4½ years. After spots appeared recently on her

See SEIDEL, Page 6C

Cancer survivor Karen Hicks hugs her son, John Hicks, after throwing out the first pitch on Friday. KIRTHMON F. DOZIER/DETROIT FREE PRESS

Willekes overcoming a new obstacle in his MSU career

Broken leg in Redbox Bowl loss puts NFL plans on hold

Chris Solari Detroit Free Press
USA TODAY NETWORK

CHICAGO – Joe Bachie ran to his fallen teammate and roommate, and his first thought was, "Oh, sh..."

He cut himself off before finishing the word, but it was clear. Seeing Kenny Willekes on the ground in pain made a seismic impression on the tough-as-nails Bachie.

In the third quarter of Michigan State's Redbox Bowl loss, Willekes laid in the end zone and told Bachie he heard a "pop." Bachie did not know the severity.

An Achilles injury? Knee? Ankle?

It took 20 minutes or so for Willekes to learn the diagnosis – a broken left fibula – and to return to the Levi's Stadium sideline, hobbling toward the Spartans' defense on crutches and with his lower leg in a walking boot.

Meanwhile, the game remained ongoing and tight, an eventual 7-6 loss to Oregon that mirrored the rest of MSU's season – a dominant defensive performance coupled with an inept offensive output.

Defensive coaches were making adjustments, players dialed in to what they were saying. And Willekes, already morphing into coaching mode, leaned in toward Bachie.

See MSU, Page 2C

Michigan State senior Kenny Willekes was the Big Ten's defensive lineman of the year in 2018. KIRTHMON F. DOZIER/DETROIT FREE PRESS

This page is from the Detroit Free Press 20th anniversary of Barry Sanders' retirement.

Except for one game in Jacksonville, I'd averaged only 3.8 yards a carry or less in the final six games of the season. Nothing was clicking. I missed my fifth consecutive 1,500-yard season by nine yards. Herman Moore missed a 1,000-yard receiving year. Robert Porcher didn't get his 13th sack.

"The thing that is most prevalent is disappointment," I told reporters after the Ravens game. "And really, just almost regret. It's almost like you wasted a whole year of football. That's how I feel right now."

A teammate, wide receiver Johnny Morton, said essentially the same thing: "It has been kind of emotionally draining. Like a really rough ride. I'm more drained than anything I've ever been through in my life, really. It seems like every aspect of football has been taken to the limit this year, from the mental approach to the game, to the schemes, to people trying to mesh together, everything."

I'd been through bad seasons before, but this was different. Everything around me told me it was time to move on. I hate to use the word burnout, but that's basically what it was. As I got older, I just didn't need it. I didn't desire it. I didn't get the same charge out of playing.

I took time in the off-season to let those feelings pass, to let the frustrations subside. Bobby Ross had given me a June 1 deadline to let him know if I would be playing or not, but that deadline came and went without a word from me. He took my silence to mean I would be returning.

> Looking back, I could have done things differently, but at the time, I wasn't trying to be diplomatic. I was trying to get my message out that I was finished, and I wasn't trying to make friends.

I didn't do anything unethical or illegal, but you couldn't tell that from the way it was covered in the media. They were unhappy with my silence, especially after the formal announcement was released, but I didn't have anything more to say than what

I'd said in my statement. There's only one thing I would have changed: I would have wished my team good luck.

Do I regret not returning the coach's phone calls? Not really. It wasn't anything against him, but at that point, nothing was going to change the circumstances, and I wasn't going to lead him on. I'd said everything I needed to say. I didn't have anything else to tell him. Maybe I should have told him that. Maybe he would have appreciated it. But for the most part, I don't regret the way I handled things.

My retirement letter didn't even hint at my frustration, because I didn't want to take shots at people as I left. I just wanted to walk away. The previous drafts of that letter, however, reeked of my general frustration. Management had let quality players slip away. We'd been losing for years. We were right back where we were when I arrived. I'd played for a period of time, in which I felt I'd experienced everything in the game I was meant to experience with that organization.

It also was the right time for me. I didn't see what good there was in hanging around, when the organization wasn't trying to put together a winning team.

Looking at what other teams in our division had done—teams such as Green Bay, which had brought in Reggie White, as well as Minnesota and Tampa Bay—I didn't think we were as serious about winning as our competitors.

PUBLIC REACTION

Even though my frustration with the organization, the loss of my former teammates and my general feeling of exhaustion, all combined to fuel my decision to retire—and those seemed like clear and valid reasons—people began inventing other reasons without knowing the truth. To some people, particularly in the media, my retirement was seen as a ploy for money, as if I was only pretending to retire so the Lions would give me a new contract. Mitch Album of the *Detroit Free Press* suggested as much. Most of what Mitch had said about me over the years was flattering, but some things he said after I retired were, for lack of a better word, interesting to me. I heard him talking about my retirement on the ESPN morning show, *The Sports Reporters*. I had always liked the commentary on the show and tried to catch it whenever possible.

During one show, they discussed my retirement, and I remember laughing and thinking to myself, "Where are these guys coming from?" Mitch made the point that whenever you hear a guy saying that it's not about money, it's always about money. Then he referred to me. I thought, "Is this the same Mitch I've known for 10 years, saying that about me? Wow." The bad part was I thought he knew me better. Years later, he said he felt strange as he heard himself making that statement. He realized what he said wasn't true.

Another explanation I often heard was that I didn't care about the game. Because I don't outwardly show my feelings, some people thought I wasn't passionate about football. To prove their theory, they often pointed to the fact that I just handed the ball to the official in the end zone after I scored a touchdown. But the way I see it, my accomplishment was crossing the goal line. I didn't have to stand back and admire it.

Everyone saw the play. I didn't feel the need to put it in everybody's face. I didn't mind celebrations. They just weren't me. I even appreciated the end zone celebrations of guys like Billy "White Shoes" Johnson when I was a kid. But everybody started doing it, and it got old. Before, it was just a couple of guys who did it. It seemed like everybody had a whole choreographed little kick-ball change thing they did.

Those things are cool, but they should never overshadow the game. It is still a team sport. Whatever you did, you had some help doing it. If I was in the Olympics, running the 100 meters, that would be a whole other ballgame. But football is a team sport, and I've always thought of it that way. I felt like the weakest link should go out and practice and play as if he's just as responsible as anyone else, and that's how you win—not by pointing the finger at somebody else or trying to grab all the glory for yourself.

No, I didn't dance around the end zone after touchdowns, but I did love scoring them, and as I've said throughout this book, I love football. For most of my life, it was a huge part of my life.

Yet another reason people (who don't even know me) gave for me leaving, was I wanted to leave the game before getting hurt. That's not true. I never said—or thought—I've got to get out while I'm healthy. I think it just kind of worked out that way. I always knew there were inherent risks in the game, and I could have the same injury as anyone else who has played.

But because I was a running back, I could only deteriorate so much before I couldn't play anyway. If I was hurting or deteriorating, they would have to get someone else in my position. At the same time, I'm the type of person who feels that if I'm too banged up, or if the game is causing too much pain and suffering on a daily basis, I won't continue.

But I've learned through the years, you have to let people say what they want and do your best to figure out the truth for yourself. When I announced my retirement, some people didn't even try to find a reason.

They were just angry. I mostly was criticized for not holding a press conference and for retiring by fax. Some letters were less than complimentary.

A guy named Jeff Primmer, from De Moines, wrote: "I have been a Detroit Lions (and subsequently, a Barry) fan for more than 40 years. How can Mr. Sanders claim the Lions teammates and coaches had been like a family to him? Who would do such a thing to his family? … I don't begrudge Mr. Sanders his personal life. I do take particular exception to the callous, selfish, backstabbing way he treated his 'friends' and 'family.' I'd hate to experience his attitude toward those he doesn't like."

On the other hand, some people rose to my defense. George Pearson, of Wichita, wrote: "I have come to believe that Mr. Sanders is a man of unusual character. Many athletes are addicted to the adulation of their fans. In turn, fans come to feel that they own a piece of that athlete. It is a dependency relationship that Sanders is having no part of … To quote a speaker that I heard recently, 'Honor is a gift that a man can only give to himself, and no other man can take that away.' That speaker could have been talking about Barry Sanders."

NO REGRETS

People ask me if I ever regret leaving, and the answer is no. For a while, I regretted the Lions—after forcing me to return a $7-million signing bonus—still retained my rights. It would have been nice to play in a Super Bowl. Had we kept some of the players we traded away, we might have gotten there, and I would have liked to get there with those guys, as a Lion.

The man with whom I had the most trouble was Chuck Schmidt. He was basically a business man who came from a very traditional background. He had his favorites, whom he'd pay, and others, whom he didn't want to pay. He is no longer part of the organization. All in all, I'm not the least bit bitter about my career and feel only good things about the Lions. In the years since my retirement, I've re-established my connection with The Lions and with the League. I have been a regular at home games and I've traveled the world representing the NFL.

Part of me wants to believe my leaving helped the organization, forcing them to go in a different direction. As long as I was there, I'd fill most of the seats and sell a lot of jerseys, even during terrible seasons. From a business standpoint, there was no reason to make a change. But with me gone, they were forced to regroup, and look at what they did after I left. My Lions wandered the NFL wilderness after my retirement. But, for the first time in many years, people are picking the Lions to win the division and to make a deep run into the playoffs.

I enjoy success in my own way, and even though we never got to the Super Bowl, I enjoyed playing. For years, people asked if I'd consider coming back. It was as if no one believed me when I explained why I retired. I retired just short of my birthday and despite what you may have heard, I never looked back. I still watch football. College, pro, whatever. I like watching a good game. But I achieved great success as a player, because I always wanted to see what I could do next, and right now, I'm interested in what I can do as a man, as a father, as a businessman and as a golfer. While I was with the Lions, I pretty much did everything that was physically possible. I don't know what else I could have done.

My father said I had no idea what kind of genuine joy I brought to people who watched me. I'd always told myself football was just a game, it really didn't matter in the grand scheme of things, but it had become more than a game in my life. True, it had helped me do wonderful things for myself, my family and my community, but it had become more than a game, and that was a problem. As I said, I'd been running on fumes for years. Those feelings had overtaken me the way night falls. It is hard to attach a time to the actual sunset, but there's no mistaking when all the light is gone.

CAREER STATS

	Rushing					Receiving			
Year	**G**	**Att**	**Yards**	**Y/A**	**TD**	**Rec**	**Yards**	**Y/R**	**TD**
1989	15	280	1,470	5.2	14	24	282	11.8	0
1990	16	255	1,304	5.1	13	36	480	13.3	3
1991	15	342	1,548	4.5	16	41	307	7.5	1
1992	16	312	1,352	4.3	9	29	225	7.8	1
1993	11	243	1,115	4.6	3	36	205	5.7	0
1994	16	331	1,883	5.7	7	44	283	6.4	1
1995	16	314	1,500	4.8	11	48	398	8.3	1
1996	16	307	1,553	5.1	11	24	147	6.1	0
1997	16	335	2,053	6.1	11	33	305	9.2	3
1998	16	343	1,491	4.3	4	37	289	7.8	0
TOTAL	**153**	**3,062**	**15,269**	**5.0**	**99**	**352**	**2,921**	**8.3**	**10**

June 27, 1999

Shortly after the end of the last season, I felt that I probably would not return for the 1999-2000 season. I also felt that I should take as much time as possible to sort through my feelings and make sure that my feelings were backed with conviction. Today, I officially declare my departure from the NFL.

It was a wonderful experience to play in the NFL, and I have no regrets. I truly will miss playing for the Lions. I consider the Lions' players, coaches, staff, management and fans my family. I leave on good terms with everyone in the organization. I have enjoyed playing for two great head coaches, Wayne Fontes and Bobby Ross, who are good coaches and leaders. I am not involved in a salary dispute of any kind. If I had played this season, I would have earned a more than satisfactory salary.

The reason I am retiring is simple: My desire to exit the game is greater than my desire to remain in it. I have searched my heart through and through, and feel comfortable with this decision.

I want to thank all of the fans and media who make playing in the NFL such a wonderful experience. I have had the pleasure of meeting many of them. Although I was not able to honor many of your requests for autographs and interviews, it was not because I overlooked the importance of those who asked.

Finally, I want to thank my family and friends for their support and guidance. I wish my teammates, coaches and the entire Lions organization all the best.

Thanks

Sincerely,

Barry Sanders
Pro Football Hall of Fame – Class of 2004
1988 Heisman Trophy Winner

www.BarrySanders.com

My retirement statement was released exclusively to the Wichita Eagle on July 27, 1999.

CHAPTER SIXTEEN

My Spiritual Walk

Most of my life has revolved around Sundays. As a player in the NFL, I made my living on Sunday afternoons. As a child, I learned about eternal life at church on Sundays. Back then, it sometimes felt as if I had spent an eternity in church, felt like I was born there. The spiritual beliefs I learned through the church remain a large part of my life.

Mother got us up early on those mornings, scrubbing us and dressing us for Sunday school. After Sunday school, we went to church for services. After a break, we returned to the church for an evening service. At various times, we sang in the choir, served on the usher board and attended a mid-week service.

During the summer, Mother organized a vacation bible school for us and all our friends. She still runs a Bible school today.

Mother was the main force that shaped my faith, and I was lucky to have her. She influenced me perhaps more than my time in church. I had such a good example at home of what a Christian should be, and I saw that example everyday.

Our church, Paradise Baptist, was led by a wonderful minister, Rev. Paul Gray. I had a lot of respect and admiration for Rev. Gray, and I remember wanting to grow up to be a preacher. We even held pretend services in our living room, with me as a preacher and my sisters as the choir and congregation.

I don't quite remember what I said, but I remember trying to mimic the flashy ministers I had seen preaching, charismatic men with stylish suits and white leather shoes.

I loved the way they dressed and the way they held everyone's attention. Rev. Gray was not that type, but I found him interesting. I didn't always appreciate all the time in the pews, however, which I guess is pretty normal for a kid. Sometimes, sitting through those long services was as much about survival as it was about revival.

But as a young man, I found a measure of sanctuary and comfort in my faith, a sound-proof bunker where I would retreat from pressures. It gave me a way of looking at things and handling them. As I've grown older, I've come to realize it's more important what you do when you're not in church, but the message of the church is still very valuable to me. When I was playing football, that message insulated me from much of the madness that surrounds a professional athlete. It kept me grounded.

Life as a professional athlete means a daily assault on your character. You're constantly being tested. At every strata of society, there's a desire for more money, more fame, more status. It is not difficult to find yourself becoming the perception others have of you. All of the temptations you can imagine swirl around you every day in that world. The principles of my faith helped me survive in that world before I was prepared for it. I had a certain amount of grounding that helped me remember who I was raised to be and who I should try to be. I felt fortunate to be in the NFL and enjoying a lot of success, and I tried to be thankful for those blessings.

However, I never wanted to set myself up as the moral conscience for the sports world, but that role eventually became my identity, particularly in the media. It seemed more important to people that I be the person they needed me to be—the refreshing alternative to the modern, narcissistic athlete—than to be myself, an imperfect human being with flaws just like everyone else.

One situation that made news was the birth of my first child. I had just finished making an abstinence video for teenagers with pro basketball star A.C. Greene, when news surfaced I had a son, but not a wife. My son, B.J. Sanders, arrived in 1994.

His mother and I dated in college and lost touch, and then we

Paradise Baptist, the church the Sanders children went to as they grew up is shown.

began seeing each other again. As I said, I had talked about no sex before marriage and had a certain image with the public, and I didn't hold a press conference to say I had crossed that line. I didn't make a practice of calling press conferences.

It may sound strange, but I don't regret anything. I love being B.J.'s dad. Although it wasn't an ideal situation or the way it was supposed to be, I knew I was taking on the biggest responsibility and the biggest privilege of my life. I had wanted to be a dad, because I came from such a big family. Family was important to me. I was shocked by the news, but I was happy about it, too. It would have been great to have been married when he was born, but when I look back, I wouldn't change a thing.

I think my parents were surprised when they heard about the situation, but they handled it well. They were very supportive. After that, the most compelling emotion I felt was the desire to be a good parent. Since the beginning, I've searched for ways to be the best possible parent. I've gotten wiser, and I'm still trying to be a better person. I hope my effort and wisdom will be reflected in the lives of my children and grandchildren.

There have been times when holding to the spiritual path that had been lit for me was difficult, and my spiritual obligations began to feel heavy. My solid family upbringing, values and principles—learned at church and at home—have guided and supported me. I'd hate to see how my life would have looked without that grace and guidance.

SHIRLEY SANDERS CELEBRATED FOR 40 YEARS OF LEADERSHIP AT VACATION BIBLE SCHOOL

The Sanders family's small, green home on North Volutsia has doubled as a kind of farm. The yield though, hasn't been measured in bushels, but instead in blessings, and the farmer has been none other than Shirley Sanders.

Last summer, Mrs. Sanders celebrated 40 growing seasons of vacation Bible school, and for a week, dozens of her former pupils crowded her driveway for cookies, Kool-Aid and testimony. We judge this agronomist on what she produces, and Mrs. Sanders has produced generations of good people.

Shontai Mouton, who attended vacation Bible school faithfully,

Barry Sanders is shown with his mother, Shirley, in front of his statue, outside the Boone Pickens football stadium at Oklahoma State University in Stillwater, Okla., in October 2021, a year before her 40th anniversary Vacation Bible School celebration.

due to her friendship with Barry's sister, Donna, said the harvest during the week-long celebration stunned her. One graduate now works as general counsel for the Department of Energy.

Another graduate, a "bad little boy whose nose always seemed runny," had grown up to become a minister, Mouton said.

"It just blew me away," said Mouton, a former IRS agent and current executive with an oil company. "He had the most beautiful testimony. He felt like (vacation Bible school) led him into the clergy."

North Volutsia's soil proved particularly rich. Every home along Volutsia, Stadium, Shadybrook and Erie streets teemed with children. You might see a new face playing bumper pool at the Lynette Woodard Community Center, and then see that child sitting next to you at vacation Bible school.

Mrs. Sanders, Mouton said, packed great efficiency into the classes, adding subtle lessons about manners and courtesy as the children were taught "please and thank you" as they passed items around.

During the celebration, Mrs. Sanders received a key to the city, and referred to her returning students as "her children." "I'll continue to pray for you and that you would continue to pray for me," she said.

Here on Kansas' windswept plains, where molten summers and arctic cold fight to a standoff, tilling, planting and harvesting makes for difficult work, but like a tree planted by the water, Mrs. Sanders would not be moved.

She raised 11 kids in her own home, and has raised dozens more in the community around her home, feeding all comers the bread of life. She left no area fallow.

And we don't need to ask what kind of agronomist she's been. We can tell this tree by the fruit it bears.

CHAPTER SEVENTEEN

Life After Football

I heard an older and wiser NFL retiree, former Minnesota Viking great and former state Supreme Court justice Alan Page, describe a football career as a suspension in time. Not a suspension of real time, but a suspension of a lifetime. Your life is, in a way, on hold.

Professional sports careers demand preparatory fidelity. As your career moves from the improbable in Little League to the possible in college, success demands intense work and focus—not simply long hours in the weight room, but on the track and on the stadium stairs.

It also requires attention to flexibility and diet. You have to learn the game on a different level, as a student, too. You need to learn to read defenses, not only for when you take the ball and run headlong into them, but so you will be better able to recognize a blitz and have to put your helmet in the chest of a charging linebacker or safety to protect your quarterback.

It is year-round work. You need to stay fit at the minimum during the off-season, but many players try to gain ground or sustain high performance through a lung-busting program. Walter Payton and Jerry Rice had legendary programs, in which they sprinted through deep sand or ran miles uphill, over rough and winding terrain.

Those workouts contributed not only to their unbelievable on-field achievements, but also to their longevity and dearth of injury. They managed to forge bodies that were gridiron tough through their workouts.

Over time, I noticed changes in my own health habits, especially with my diet. As the healthcare industry issued many warnings about sugar and fat consumption, I could have been their poster boy. As I mentioned already, early in my career, the night before a game, you'd find me heading to my hotel room with a brown grocery sack full of all manner of sweets and confections, including my Suzy Q's. I didn't know at the time how this diet impacted my weight.

More than halfway through my career, I knew I needed to make some changes, in order to boost my performance. I'd been putting up good numbers every year, but I took a lot of playful ribbing, particularly from Herman Moore, our All-Pro wide receiver, for getting caught from behind by defenders on some of my longer runs. I knew I wasn't the best I could be, and there was room for improvement.

I noticed some other aspects of form and function I hoped to improve, particularly my knee lift and my heel turnover. While watching game film, I noticed when I was in full stride, my knees didn't piston very high. It didn't need to be as high as San Francisco 49ers great Roger Craig's chest-high lift, but I certainly had room to improve. I also noticed my turnover—how close my heels came to my butt while in stride—wasn't very good either.

These inefficiencies probably robbed me of some speed and some performance. To improve myself, to stretch my boundaries (and also to properly finish off those long runs), I had to make some changes. I started with my diet. I traded in my Suzy Q's and sack-loads of candy for platefuls of fresh vegetables and more salads with less dressing.

I also started a stretching regimen to increase my flexibility and improve my form. Compare game film from early in my career to later footage, and you see a slimmer me with a higher knee lift and more efficient turnover. You see I'm finishing runs on my feet in the end zone, as opposed to being dragged down from behind.

I always put everything into my preparation and was pleased to see it pay off on the field. I worked hard during the season, as well as during the off-season, to meet all of the physical challenges of facing stubborn defenses dug in to stop me. I saw the benefits of such hard work in the various successes I had on the field, but over time, I felt the routine draining me, in the same way a bad relationship can be draining. It wasn't simply the workouts (I've always loved physical activity), but a little of everything. I was putting far more into my career physically and emotionally than I was receiving professionally.

That's when I started thinking about what Alan Page had said about a pro career representing a suspension in time. Living in this way can distort your view of what constitutes a responsible adult life. You can decide to grow up, or you can remain dependent on the system to take care of you.

You have that choice. The price of that choice, however, is allowing your life to be structured and controlled by other people.

So I left on my own terms, and I'm living on my own terms. Some players see the final year of their careers as an ending, and in some cases careers end before the person is ready to move on. In my case, it ended when I was ready. I felt it was a beginning, opening up many more possibilities for my life, and I felt confident about what lay ahead.

THE ROAD AHEAD

Since retiring from the game, I have been doing some of the things everyone else does, such as investing in business, trying to better manage my earnings, caring for my mother, raising kids. I'm involved in developing a host of business ventures, which keep me busy. I'm also doing some of the things most people don't get a chance to do, such as travel when and where I want, as well as playing all the holes of golf I want.

Golf has been a special retirement boon, and I've been playing in celebrity tournaments, such as Tiger Jam. I'm also doing some of the things I should do. I participate in a number of charities, and I often look for ways to help people help themselves. I like to think that I'm good at balancing things and excelling at more than one thing at a time. I'm certainly trying to do that.

MY BOYS

In having my four sons, I'm fulfilling one of my father's fondest wishes that I'd someday raise a family of my own.

Barrry James (B.J.) Sanders, my oldest, was just 5 when I retired, so he did not get to see much of my career.

Then I married Lauren and I had a fruitful 10-year marriage, where we welcomed my three youngest boys, Nigel, Nicholas and Noah.

Barry Sanders and his oldest son, B.J. are shown while working as a Madden Ratings Adjustor before a Detroit Lions game.

I am so proud of B.J., who earned a communications and media studies degree from Stanford University. He then transferred to my alma mater, Oklahoma State University, where he focused on leisure studies, and followed in my footsteps as a running back for the Pokes. He's now a manager with EA Sports.

Barry Sanders is shown with his son, Nigel, after a Detroit, Symphony Orchestra, Youth Jazz Ensemble performances, when he was about 15.

Nigel is very much a renaissance man. He excelled athletically and academically and spent time performing theatrical music, playing a range of instruments including the tuba, trumpet and percussion instruments. In fact, he's quite the musician. He graduated with honors from Detroit Country Day School with the honors music conservatory designation. Nigel has worked with Detroit rappers, including current projects with Public Enemy and others, Nigel is on track to graduate from Howard University with a degree in African-American studies, with possible plans for law or graduate school.

Barry Sanders is shown with his son, Nicholas, during his senior photo shoot, in 2021.

Nicholas (Nic) was always conscientious about orginization—from his orderly clothing drawers to retiring to bed early enough to arrive 15 minutes early for appointments. Like Nigel, Nic also developed a love for music, beginning piano lessons at 4 and playing the alto saxophone in the high school orchestra. Also like Nigel, Nic excelled at the rigorous Detroit Country Day school, graduating with top academic honors, including the President's Award. Upon graduation, Nic had lots of options, but opted to accept a spot as a walk-on for legendary college basketball coach Tom Izzo at Michigan State University. He wears No. 20.

Barry Sanders is shown with his son, Noah, while playing in the yard in 2016.

Noah always had something calming and warm about him and it showed up when he saw a teacher fall at school. He rushed to her, helped lift her to her feet and then gathered her books and papers that scattered during her fall. He then helped her to her chair. Months later, with the teacher's family present, Noah received an award for his humanitarian concern. Like his brothers, Noah enjoyed flag football as well as building elaborate Lego airplanes and commercial airliners. In fact, he can fly the Microsoft flight simulator and has considered the Tuskegee Airman Detroit ground school for his pilot's license. As with his brothers, he is an accomplished musician. He's particularly talented at playing the trumpet. Turns out, he's quite an athlete, too. He set the 100-meter record at his school as a sophomore, and received an invitation to the 2023 Junior Olympics. Recently, he has been racking up the yards and touchdowns as he earns more time at running back for Birminghan Groves High School.

I'm feeling about as settled as I've ever felt in my life. I'm really getting a chance to appreciate family life and raising kids. I'm enjoying the little things. I'm not lost in being a parent.

I still make my home in Michigan for the time being. My goal is to create the best home I can for them, an environment that gives them the chance to be good people, much like the one I had way back on North Volutsia, in Wichita.

CHAPTER EIGHTEEN

Forward Progress

The administrative office that manages high school sports and other activities in my home state of Kansas recently discovered that despite National Football League ceremonies at my high school, my presence in the College Football and NFL Hall of Fames, I was not in the Kansas high school version.

Many of the folks involved felt terrible about the oversight, and planned to fast-track my induction, but my representatives, who know me well, told the state officials not to worry. In fact, we said if they pushed it a year, I might actually manage to attend the ceremony.

Recognition isn't a birthright, nor is it the salve people make it out to be. It's not that I don't appreciate awards and recognition, but rather, it's that those things do not motivate me and never have. I guess I'm a sportsmanship purist.

While I'm incredibly honored to be in the Hall of Fames, standing with some of the greats of college and the NFL, those elite groups were not the focus of why I wanted to play. I just wanted to play the game, be better than I was the previous year and enjoy the experience of the game.

As I've mentioned, various coaches over my career have asked if I wanted them to put me back in a game, in which winning was a virtual certainty, to try and secure a record. Each time—in high school, in college and in the pros—I declined.

There's something that feels artificial about setting a record that way. If I'd set a record executing our game plan, in the course of our work as a team, fine. But placing my personal success ahead of the team's success felt like a sportsmanship violation.

Barry Sanders, right, is shown with, from left, J.B. Bernstein, his agent, and Mark McCormick, his lifelong friend, during a recent event in honor of his high school football coach, Coach B.

It's the thing about me that has changed little over the years. Still, I'm enjoying life in my 50s, perhaps more than I ever have on my personal journey and I've surprised myself with what has changed. Where I have grown. What I have learned.

I'm in more commercials and I'm doing more endorsements now as a retired player than I ever did as an active player. I'm actually a ubiquitous presence in a slate of ad campaigns from MGM Grand, to Nissan's Heisman House to Rocket Mortgage, to a host of other ventures.

I'm more popular today than I ever was as an active player.

I'm also decades and miles from the anxious college student athlete, who asked one of my best friends to visit me in Stillwater, as my star rose and as thirsty talent agents descended on me as I left the practice field. My dad believed I went to Oklahoma State to hide my talent, but really, I just wanted to play ball.

I never really celebrated after a score, but that didn't mean I didn't play with passion or intensity. I could appreciate Billy White Shoes Johnson's dancing, end zone celebrations without needing to imitate him. Crossing the goal line over the efforts of players and coaches trying to stop me, felt like statement enough.

I never sought the spotlight, and I still don't. But when it lands on me today, it just doesn't land as hard as it used to. I feel comfortable now managing those tasks. I don't love all the public-facing work I do, but I don't have the same dread about it that I used to have.

I've actually worked as an NFL Ambassador, traveling to Europe and to China helping to promote football in both places.

On commercial sets, I'd like to think I have a reputation as someone who is professional, but who also operates with the type of kindness and humility that have made me easy to work with and hopefully someone who will get invited back.

That's not just a brand. That's who I am, and I'm maybe more myself than I've ever been.

Retirement had a lot to do with this personal growth. We endure a lot as players.

> We face pressurized demands on our time from family and friends, from fans, from news media, from our agents and business partners. We do this while playing a fun and rewarding, yet manifestly violent and inherently dangerous game.

My decision to retire remains a critical life inflection point.

It was one of the few times I'd made a major decision for myself, based on my feelings and what I considered the best choice for my life. I'd nursed the possibility for at least a year beforehand. I went back and forth about my responsibilities to myself, to my teammates and to my fans.

But ultimately, I chose myself and then braced myself for the bitter reaction. The venom and bile surprised me, I'd have to admit. But the biggest surprise I think came from my dad, who expressed pride in my decision (maybe because I retired the way his previous favorite player, Jim Brown, retired).

I felt as though I'd grown in stature in my father's eyes. In the aftermath of my retirement announcement, it felt like the world at once mis-characterized me as selfish or cowardly.

> My dad may have been my first and most consistent critic, from catching punts on a dead run, not letting punts hit the ground and generally accepting the responsibility of being the best player on a team. But he was almost always right, and he always said what he said out of love and concern.

After years of at times bumping heads with my dad and not fully understanding his motivations, having lost him, I find as each day, week and season pass, I have more and more in common with him and I see the genius and concern in so much of how he raised us and prepared us for life.

I'm not my dad, now that I am a dad, but I lean more and more on his wisdom and insights in my interactions with my boys. It was my dad's fondest wish that I'd someday raise a family of my own.

I have that today. I only wish he could have been around longer to see the men they're becoming.

The boys also would benefit from hearing his stories and his memories from his mouth. Learning from him how a man approaches life, family and difficulty. We miss him daily, but he left us with so many life lessons, so much grit and toughness, so much intensity.

My hope is he's proud of me and the boys. I raised them as the man he raised me to be. Not necessarily the man he wanted me to be, but the best version of me I could be. There are times when we couldn't have more dissimilar personalities, but we both have lived life on our terms.

I'm so proud of everything he and my mother gave us, from our humble beginnings to our abiding Christian faith, to our embrace of higher education. As kids, we may not have had everything we wanted, but our parents gave us everything we needed to be successful adults.

Standing on their shoulders and on their lessons, I manage several businesses. I've long been active as a philanthropist of sorts, quietly purchasing shoes, jerseys or equipment for little league teams, or as the anonymous donor who helped someone pay for college.

Those are the things that matter most. As Dr. King said, the most urgent question we face is, what are we doing to help someone else?

Perhaps that's why as another honor heads my way in the form of acknowledgment from the high school activities association in Kansas, my thought was less about celebrating another honor, but putting the people there at the association at ease, and even finding a way to help them be successful.

Bill Faflick, the executive director of the Kansas State High School Athletic Association, said his organization's Hall of Fame is the way the association honors excellence.

"Having been a part of the Wichita community for many years, including my first semester as a teacher at Wichita North (High School), I am aware of a number of individuals that may be worthy of inclusion," he said in an email. "In this particular case, I would like to nominate Barry for the NFHS Hall of Fame, but believe his case for inclusion is strengthened when he is in our HOF."

I'd like to thank Mr. Faflick and the others responsible for my nomination. I'm honored. I mean, a person could argue I ***didn't*** have a stellar high school career as a running back. I didn't start at that position until the fourth game of my senior season.

I ended that season averaging 10.2 yards per carry, but it was just one season.

That school has grown, as I have.

It has a new gym, new classrooms and the district may not be done building. I've heard there are plans to build a football stadium behind the high school, on the river. The same steep riverbank where we carried teammates on our shoulders during grueling, two-a-day practices in scorching Kansas heat.

It was tough, but all of us are better for the experience.

Just like me.

CHAPTER NINETEEN

Career at a Glance

Barry Sanders is enjoying the celebrations at the Oklahoma State football game, the weekend of the statue unveiling in Stillwater.

1989

- Gained 1,470 yards to set the team's single-season rushing mark and was second NFL rookie to set the rookie record for rushing yards, behind Eric Dickerson with 1,808 yards in 1983; both records were previously held by Billy Sims
- Scored 14 rushing touchdowns, establishing a new Detroit Lions record
- Returned five kickoffs for 118 yards (23.6 avg.)
- Named first-team All-Pro by *The Associated Press, College & Pro Football News Weekly, Pro Football Writers of America, Football Digest, Sporting News* and *Pro Football Weekly*
- Voted NFL Offensive Rookie of the Year by *Pro Football Weekly, Football Digest, College & Pro Football News Weekly* and *The Associated Press*
- Selected first-team ALL-NFC by *Football News* and *United Press International*
- NFC Rookie of the Year by *United Press International*
- Lions' Offensive MVP and the Lions' Quarterback Club Offensive MVP
- Elected to the Pro Bowl

1990

- Won the NFL rushing title with 1,304 yards on 255 carries (5.1 yards per carry average), making him the first Detroit Lion to win that title since Byron "Whizzer" White led the league in 1940
- Scored 13 rushing touchdowns, 16 in all, tying the Lions record
- Named All-pro by *The Associated Press, United Press International, Pro Football Writers of America, Pro Football Weekly, Sporting News, College & Pro Football News Weekly, Sports Illustrated's* Dr. "Z" Team and *Football News*
- Earned second appearance in the Pro Bowl
- Named the Lions' Offensive MVP and, with 96 points, became the first one-kicker to lead Detroit in scoring since Mel Farr and Bill Gambrell each tallied 42 points in 1968

1991

- Finished second in the league in rushing (to Emmit Smith of the Dallas Cowboys) with 1,548 yards, setting a Lions team record
- Led the league in touchdowns with 17
- Named the NFL Players Association NFC Most Valuable Player
- Selected *Football Digest's* NFL Player of the Year
- Won the Maxwell Football Club's Pro Player of the Year Award
- Won Consensus All-Pro honors (*The Associated Press, United Press International, Pro Football Writers of America, Pro Football Weekly, Sporting News, College & Pro Football News Weekly, Football Digest, Sports Illustrated* and *Football News*)
- Made third start in the Pro Bowl
- Named the NFC's Offensive Player of the Month for September
- Led Detroit in scoring for the second straight year
- Became the first non-kicker in team history to score more than 100 points in a season (102)

1992

- Finished second in the NFC and fourth in the NFL with 1,352 yards rushing
- Started fourth Pro Bowl
- Earned All-NFC honors from *United Press International,*

Barry Sanders is shown getting recognized during an Oklahoma State basketball game the weekend of the statue unveiling.

Football News and *Pro Football Weekly*
• Named second-team All Pro by *The Associated Press, NEA Sports Magazine* and *College & Pro Football News Weekly*
• Went over the 5,000-yard mark for career with 94 rushing yards in 24 carries at Pittsburgh
• Became the Lions all-time rushing leader after gaining 151 yards at Cincinnati

1993

• Missed the final five games of the season with a sprained knee, returning for the Wild-Card game against Green Bay to gain 169 yards on 27 carries
• Before the injury, suffered against the Chicago Bears on Thanksgiving Day, led the league in rushing with 1,052 yards
• Had only missed two previous games in his career
• Selected to start his fifth Pro Bowl, but did not play, due to injury
• Surpassed the 6,000-yard rushing mark for career, gained 90 yards against Phoenix

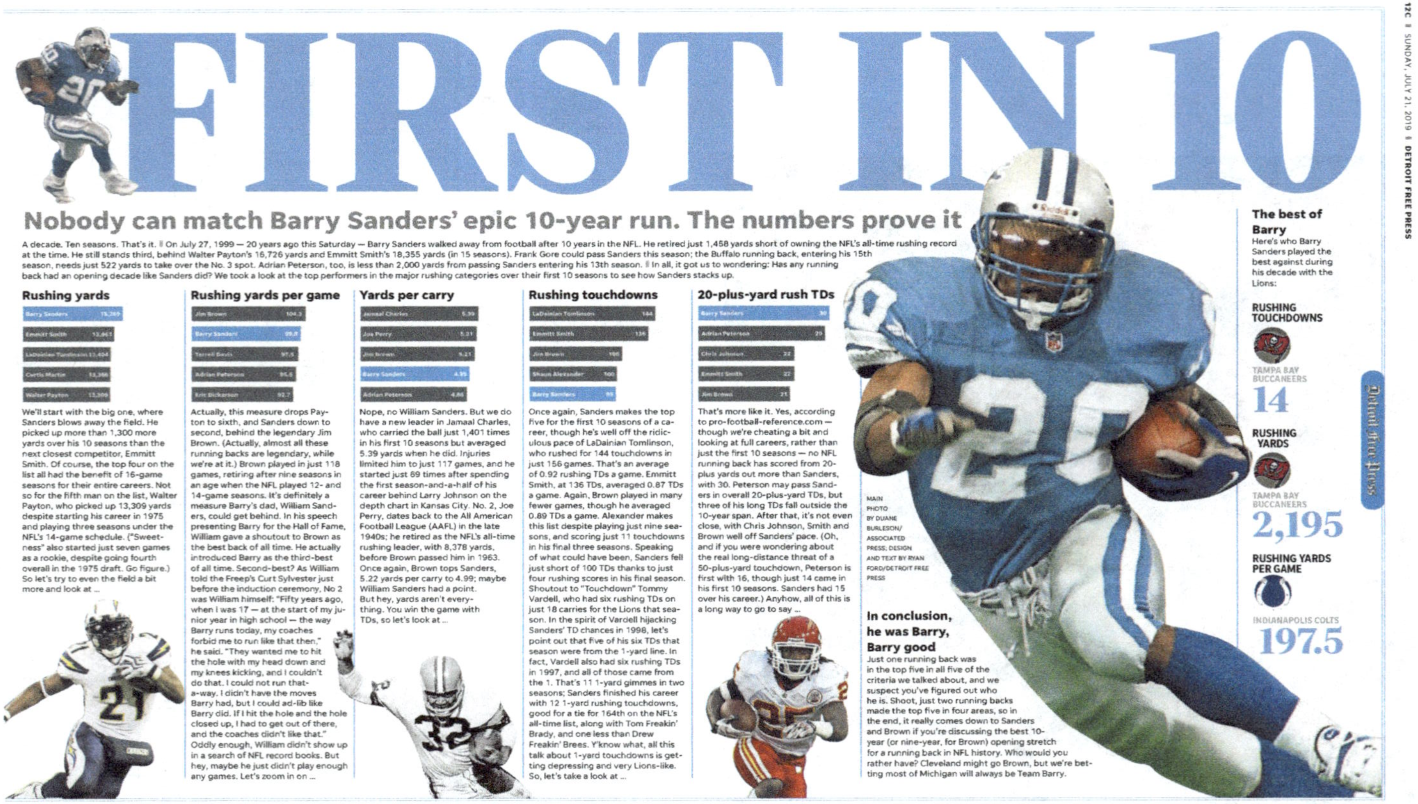

12C | SUNDAY, JULY 21, 2019 | DETROIT FREE PRESS

Detroit Free Press

FIRST IN 10

Nobody can match Barry Sanders' epic 10-year run. The numbers prove it

A decade. Ten seasons. That's it. | On July 27, 1999 — 20 years ago this Saturday — Barry Sanders walked away from football after 10 years in the NFL. He retired just 1,458 yards short of owning the NFL's all-time rushing record at the time. He still stands third, behind Walter Payton's 16,726 yards and Emmitt Smith's 18,355 yards (in 15 seasons). Frank Gore could pass Sanders this season; the Buffalo running back, entering his 15th season, needs just 522 yards to take over the No. 3 spot. Adrian Peterson, too, is less than 2,000 yards from passing Sanders entering his 13th season. | In all, it got us to wondering: Has any running back had an opening decade like Sanders did? We took a look at the top performers in the major rushing categories over their first 10 seasons to see how Sanders stacks up.

Rushing yards

Barry Sanders	15,269
Emmitt Smith	13,963
LaDainian Tomlinson	13,404
Curtis Martin	13,366
Walter Payton	13,309

We'll start with the big one, where Sanders blows away the field. He picked up more than 1,300 more yards over his 10 seasons than the next closest competitor, Emmitt Smith. Of course, the top four on the list all had the benefit of 16-game seasons for their entire careers. Not so for the fifth man on the list, Walter Payton, who picked up 13,309 yards despite starting his career in 1975 and playing three seasons under the NFL's 14-game schedule. ("Sweetness" also started just seven games as a rookie, despite going fourth overall in the 1975 draft. Go figure.) So let's try to even the field a bit more and look at ...

Rushing yards per game

Jim Brown	104.3
Barry Sanders	99.8
Terrell Davis	97.5
Adrian Peterson	95.5
Eric Dickerson	92.7

Actually, this measure drops Payton to sixth, and Sanders down to second, behind the legendary Jim Brown. (Actually, almost all these running backs are legendary, while we're at it.) Brown played in just 118 games, retiring after nine seasons in an age when the NFL played 12- and 14-game seasons. It's definitely a measure Barry's dad, William Sanders, could get behind. In his speech presenting Barry for the Hall of Fame, William gave a shoutout to Brown as the best back of all time. He actually introduced Barry as the third-best of all time. Second-best? As William told the Freep's Curt Sylvester just before the induction ceremony, No 2 was William himself: "Fifty years ago, when I was 17 — at the start of my junior year in high school — the way Barry runs today, my coaches forbid me to run like that then," he said. "They wanted me to hit the hole with my head down and my knees kicking, and I couldn't do that. I could not run that-a-way. I didn't have the moves Barry had, but I could ad-lib like Barry did. If I hit the hole and the hole closed up, I had to get out of there, and the coaches didn't like that." Oddly enough, William didn't show up in a search of NFL record books. But hey, maybe he just didn't play enough any games. Let's zoom in on ...

Yards per carry

Jamaal Charles	5.39
Joe Perry	5.31
Jim Brown	5.21
Barry Sanders	4.99
Adrian Peterson	4.86

Nope, no William Sanders. But we do have a new leader in Jamaal Charles, who carried the ball just 1,401 times in his first 10 seasons but averaged 5.39 yards when he did. Injuries limited him to just 117 games, and he started just 69 times after spending the first season-and-a-half of his career behind Larry Johnson on the depth chart in Kansas City. No. 2, Joe Perry, dates back to the All American Football League (AAFL) in the late 1940s; he retired as the NFL's all-time rushing leader, with 8,378 yards, before Brown passed him in 1963. Once again, Brown tops Sanders, 5.22 yards per carry to 4.99; maybe William Sanders had a point. But hey, yards aren't everything. You win the game with TDs, so let's look at ...

Rushing touchdowns

LaDainian Tomlinson	144
Emmitt Smith	136
Jim Brown	106
Shaun Alexander	100
Barry Sanders	99

Once again, Sanders makes the top five for the first 10 seasons of a career, though he's well off the ridiculous pace of LaDainian Tomlinson, who rushed for 144 touchdowns in just 156 games. That's an average of 0.92 rushing TDs a game. Emmitt Smith, at 136 TDs, averaged 0.87 TDs a game. Again, Brown played in many fewer games, though he averaged 0.89 TDs a game. Alexander makes this list despite playing just nine seasons, and scoring just 11 touchdowns in his final three seasons. Speaking of what could have been, Sanders fell just short of 100 TDs thanks to just four rushing scores in his final season. Shoutout to "Touchdown" Tommy Vardell, who had six rushing TDs on just 18 carries for the Lions that season. In the spirit of Vardell hijacking Sanders' TD chances in 1998, let's point out that five of his six TDs that season were from the 1-yard line. In fact, Vardell also had six rushing TDs in 1997, and all of those came from the 1. That's 11 1-yard gimmes in two seasons; Sanders finished his career with 12 1-yard rushing touchdowns, good for a tie for 164th on the NFL's all-time list, along with Tom Freakin' Brady, and one less than Drew Freakin' Brees. Y'know what, all this talk about 1-yard touchdowns is getting depressing and very Lions-like. So, let's take a look at ...

20-plus-yard rush TDs

Barry Sanders	30
Adrian Peterson	29
Chris Johnson	22
Emmitt Smith	22
Jim Brown	21

That's more like it. Yes, according to pro-football-reference.com — though we're cheating a bit and looking at full careers, rather than just the first 10 seasons — no NFL running back has scored from 20-plus yards out more than Sanders, with 30. Peterson may pass Sanders in overall 20-plus-yard TDs, but three of his long TDs fall outside the 10-year span. After that, it's not even close, with Chris Johnson, Smith and Brown well off Sanders' pace. (Oh, and if you were wondering about the real long-distance threat of a 50-plus-yard touchdown, Peterson is first with 16, though just 14 came in his first 10 seasons. Sanders had 15 over his career.) Anyhow, all of this is a long way to go to say ...

MAIN PHOTO BY DUANE BURLESON/ASSOCIATED PRESS; DESIGN AND TEXT BY RYAN FORD/DETROIT FREE PRESS

In conclusion, he was Barry, Barry good

Just one running back was in the top five in all five of the criteria we talked about, and we suspect you've figured out who he is. Shoot, just two running backs made the top five in four areas, so in the end, it really comes down to Sanders and Brown if you're discussing the best 10-year (or nine-year, for Brown) opening stretch for a running back in NFL history. Who would you rather have? Cleveland might go Brown, but we're betting most of Michigan will always be Team Barry.

The best of Barry

Here's who Barry Sanders played the best against during his decade with the Lions:

RUSHING TOUCHDOWNS
TAMPA BAY BUCCANEERS
14

RUSHING YARDS
TAMPA BAY BUCCANEERS
2,195

RUSHING YARDS PER GAME
INDIANAPOLIS COLTS
197.5

This page is from the Detroit Free Press 20th anniversary of Barry Sanders' retirement.

• Ran for what was then the second-highest rushing total of his career with 187 yards in 29 carries vs. Tampa Bay, earning NFL Player of the Week by the *Pro Football Writers of America* and NFC Offensive Player of the Week
• Surpassed the 1,000-yard mark for the fifth time in as many seasons with 75 yards on 17 carries at Green Bay

1994

• Named NFL Player of the Year by *Football Digest*
• Chosen first-team All-Pro by *Sporting News, USA Today, College & Pro Football News Weekly, Football Digest, Pro Football Weekly, Pro Football Writers of America* and *Sports Illustrated*
• Named *The Associated Press* Offensive Player of the Year
• Set a then-career-high rushing total with 1,883-yards, the fourth-highest single-season rushing total in the NFL history at the time
• Set a Lions' single-game record and a career high with 237 yards against Tampa Bay
• All-NFC first-team pick by *Football News* and *United Press International*
• Named NFL Players Association NFC Most Valuable Player
• Won the 1994 ESPN "Espy" Award for NL Performer of the Year
• Voted NFC Player-of-the-Month for October, NFC Offensive Player of the Week (Weeks 3, 10 and 16)
• Surpassed the 7,000-yard mark for career with 194 yards in a career high 40 carries at Dallas (those 40 carries are the most ever gained against the Cowboys)
• Made the longest run of his career at Tampa Bay, on 85-yarder, after losing shoe on the play
• Made an 84-yard run against Chicago the longest in Silverdome history and the second-longest of career at the time
• Surpassed the 10,000-yard mark in career total yardage against the Packers
• Limited to only 52 yards against Miami on Christmas Day, falling short in the quest for 2,000 yards
• Led team with seven catches for 58 yards against the Dolphins
• Held to minus one yard rushing, a career-low, on 13 carries and caught three passes for four yards in the Wild-Card game at Green Bay

1995

• Named to NFC's starting Pro Bowl squad for the seventh season
• Rushed for 1,500 yards
• Finished with a career-high 48 receptions for 398 yards and one touchdown
• Named first-team All-Pro by *The Associated Press, College & Pro Football News Weekly, Football Digest, Pro Football Weekly, Pro Football Writers of America, Sporting News* and *Sports Illustrated*
• Named All-NFC first-team by *Football News* and *United Press International*
• All-Madden Team member and NFC Offensive Player of the Week for games vs. Green Bay (10/15)
• Tied career-high with nine receptions (for 60 yards) against Minnesota
• The streak of 803 consecutive attempts (703 rushes and 100 receptions) without a turnover was broken in the fourth quarter against Arizona
• Made the longest scoring run of career at the time, 75 yards, against Cleveland
• Rushed for a season-high 167 yards on 22 carries against Green Bay
• Scored two touchdowns and rushed for 120 yards against Chicago, surpassing the 1,000-yard mark for the season, becoming one of only two backs (Eric Dickerson is the other) in NFL history to rush for over 1,000 yards in each of their first seven seasons at the time
• Rushed for 54 yards at Houston (12/10), surpassing the 10,000-yard mark for career (10th player in NFL history)
• Had 10 carries for 40 yards and caught two passes for 19 yards in Wild Card game against Philadelphia

1996

• Won third NFL rushing title in dramatic fashion, gaining 175 yards at San Francisco in the final game of the season, totaling 1,553 yards, then the second-highest season total in his career
• Eighth consecutive 1,000-yard season, broke NFL record to begin career, previously held by Eric Dickerson

• Became the first player in NFL history to rush for 1,500 yards in three consecutive years
• Selected as a starter in Pro Bowl for eighth year
• Selected All Pro by *Pro Football Weekly, Pro Football Writers of America* and *Sporting News*
• Named second-team All-Pro by *College & Pro Football News Weekly, United Press International, The Associated Press* and *Football Digest*

1997

• Named NFL MVP by *Pro Football Writers of America, Sporting News, Pro Football Weekly, Football Digest, Sports Illustrated* and *The Maxwell Club*
• Named Miller Lite Player of the Year
• Named co-MVP by *The Associated Press*
• Named NFL Offensive Player of the Year by *The Associated Press* and *College & Pro Football News Weekly*
• Became the third player in NFL history to rush for more than 2,000 yards in a season (2,053 yards), joining Eric Dickerson (2,105 in 1984) and O.J. Simpson (2,003 in 1973)
• Moved into second-place on NFL's all-time rushing list with 13,778 yards, trailing only Walter Payton
• Set an NFL record for most 100-yard games in a season with 14 (also a record for consecutive 100-yard games)
• Recorded 100-plus yards in all eight road games, establishing an NFL record 10 such consecutive outings (dating back to 1996)
• Formed with wide receiver Herman Moore the first duo from the same team since 1954 to either win or share (Moore tied with Oakland's Tim Brown) league rushing and receiving titles the same season
• Surpassed the 1,500-yard mark for the fifth time, establishing a league record he had shared with Walter Payton and Eric Dickerson
• Became the first player in NFL history to post two 80-yard touchdown runs in one game (80 and 82 yards against Tampa Bay) and three
80-yard touchdown runs in a single season (an 80-yarder against Indianapolis)
• Selected first-team All-Pro by *The Associated Press, Sports Illustrated, Pro Football Weekly, College & Pro Football News*

Weekly, Sporting News, Football Digest and *USA Today*
• Earned NFC Offensive Player of the Month award for October, November and December, becoming the first NFL player to capture the award in consecutive months since Steve Young in November and December of 1994, and first ever to win the award three times in a single season
• After being held to 53 yards in 25 carries in the season's first two games, reached 100 yards in every remaining regular season game
• Recorded second career 100-yard game vs. Tampa Bay (9/7) with season-high eight catches for 102 yards
• Held to 65 yards on 18 carries in Wild Card playoff game at Tampa Bay

1998

• Rushed for 1,491 yards and four touchdowns in team-record 343 carries en route to tenth Pro Bowl selection
• Had 343 attempts on the year, broke own team recored (342 carries in 1991)
• Fell nine yards short of becoming the first player in NFL history to rush for 1,500 yards in five consecutive seasons (already the only player in history with five overall)
• Named second-team All-Pro by *The Associated Press*
• Rushed for 100 yards in five consecutive weeks, the second-longest streak of 100-yard games in career
• Two all-time NFL streaks halted in season opener at Green Bay—most consecutive 100-yard rushing games (14) and most consecutive 100-yard rushing games on the road (10)
• Rushed for 155 yards against Green Bay, including a 73 yarder for a touchdown, representing the 25th time exceeded 150 and the 15th time scored a touchdown with a run exceeding 50 yards, and both were NFL records at the time
• Gained 140 yards against Philadelphia to surpass 1,000 yards for the season, and the 10th time in his career, which tied the record held by Walter Payton
• Became the second player in NFL history to exceed 15,000 rushing yards, and the third player to go over the 18,000 total yardage mark
• Moved into second-place on the NFL all-time total yardage list, passing Herschel Walker.

CHAPTER TWENTY

Photos

Left: Barry Sanders dances with his niece, Nia Simpson, during his wedding reception in November 2000.

Bottom left: Barry Sanders is shown with his youngest son, Noah Sanders.

Bottom right: Barry Sanders is shown with two of his sons, B.J. Sanders and Nigel Sanders.

Above left: Byron Sanders, William Boyd Sanders, Barry Sanders and their mother, Shirley Sanders, are shown in the living room of the Sanders Home. **Above right:** Barry Sanders is shown with his son, Nigel, after one of Nigel's Detroit Symphony Orchestra Youth Jazz Ensemble performances.

Above: Impromptu family photo in Canton, Ohio, the year Barry Sanders was inducted into the NFL Hall of Fame. Fourth row standing, from left, are Miles (in his father's arms), Marcus Phillips, Aunt Alverta Phillips, Elaine Sanders, Aunt Johnnie Mae Gandy, Adrianne Scott, Credrick Scott, Zara Scott (in her father's arms); third row standing, from left, are Diane (Sanders) Criner, Aunt Joyce Drake, Lynn Sanders, Myles Hall (in Lynn's arms), Nick Sanders (in his mother's arms), Lauren Sanders, Gloria Sanders, Krista Sanders, Gina (Sanders) Hall, Donald Drake Jr.; second row standing, from left, are Andrew Sanders Aaron Simpson, Nia Simpson, Hazel Sanders, Dedra Sanders (kneeling), B.J. Sanders, Gary Hall; and front row sitting, from left, are William Sanders, Shirley Sanders, Barry Sanders, Nigel Sanders (in his father's lap), Byron Sanders, William Boyd Sanders and Tarik Simpson (standing on the end).

Above: Barry Sanders is shown holding his oldest son, B.J., at his sister's wedding. **Left:** Barry Sanders is shown with his son, Nigel, who played an instrument throughout his high school career and graduated with Honors Conservatory for piano/trumpet/tuba/percussion.

Above: Barry Sanders is shown with his mother, Shirley Sanders, at his wedding, while she is giving her blessings over his life. **Left:** Barry Sanders is shown with Nicholas Sanders, Demetria Sanders, Gloria Sanders Gina Hall, Krista Sanders, Myles Hall, Lynn Sanders, Maya Hall, Lauren Sanders and Nigel Sanders at Thanksgiving in Montgomery, Ala.

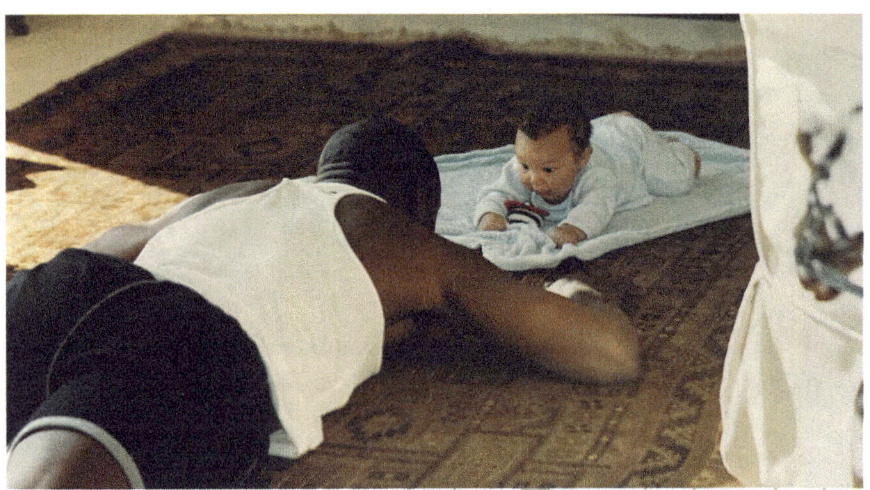

Above: Barry Sanders is shown with his son, Nic. **Right:** Barry Sanders' sons, Nic, Noah and Nigel are shown in Miami, Fla., during a family trip. **Below:** Family members gather for a photo in the family room at their home on Volutsia. Shown in the back row, from left, are Boyd Sanders, Byron Sanders, Nancy Sanders, Gina Hall; in the second row, from left, are Diane Criner, Krista Sanders, Emmanuel Criner, Donna Sanders, Elaine Sanders, in the third row, from left, are Barry Sanders, Lynn Sanders, Gloria Sanders; and in the front row, from left, are Adrian Sanders, Demetria Sanders.

Krista Sanders is shown playing around with her brother, Barry Sanders.

Above: Barry Sanders is shown with his sons, Noah, B.J. and Nigel after one of B.J.'s football games at Oklahoma State. **Left:** Family members are shown at their childhood home on Volutsia. Pictured in the back row standing, from left, are Diane Sanders (Criner), Nancy Sanders, Boyd Sanders, Lynn Sanders, William Sanders, Byron Sanders.; in the middle Row seated, from left, are Elaine Sanders, Shirley Sanders, Gloria Sanders; in the front row seated, from left, are Barry Sanders, Krista Sanders, Donna Sanders (Simpson) and Gina Sanders (Hall).

Above: Barry Sanders is shown with his sons B.J., Nigel, Nic and Noah after Nic's graduation. **Right:** Nic taking tour of Michigan Statue University facilities with former star player in front of his "kiss" tradition photo. **Below:** B.J. Sanders announces where he will attend college at the Army All American football game. Pictured are James Sr., Barry, James Jr., Nigel, Terrance, Barry J., Aletha and Sampson.

Top left: Barry Sanders' son, Noah, dressed as his dad for Halloween on year. **Top right:** Barry Sanders is shown with his son, Noah, in Florida, a common vacation spot. **Middle left:** Nic is shown during a ceremony where he received an academic excellence Presidential Award. **Middle right:** Barry Sanders is shown with family after Nigel's high school graduation party. **Left:** Barry Sanders is shown taking a breather at the Jeep NFL Allstar weekend.

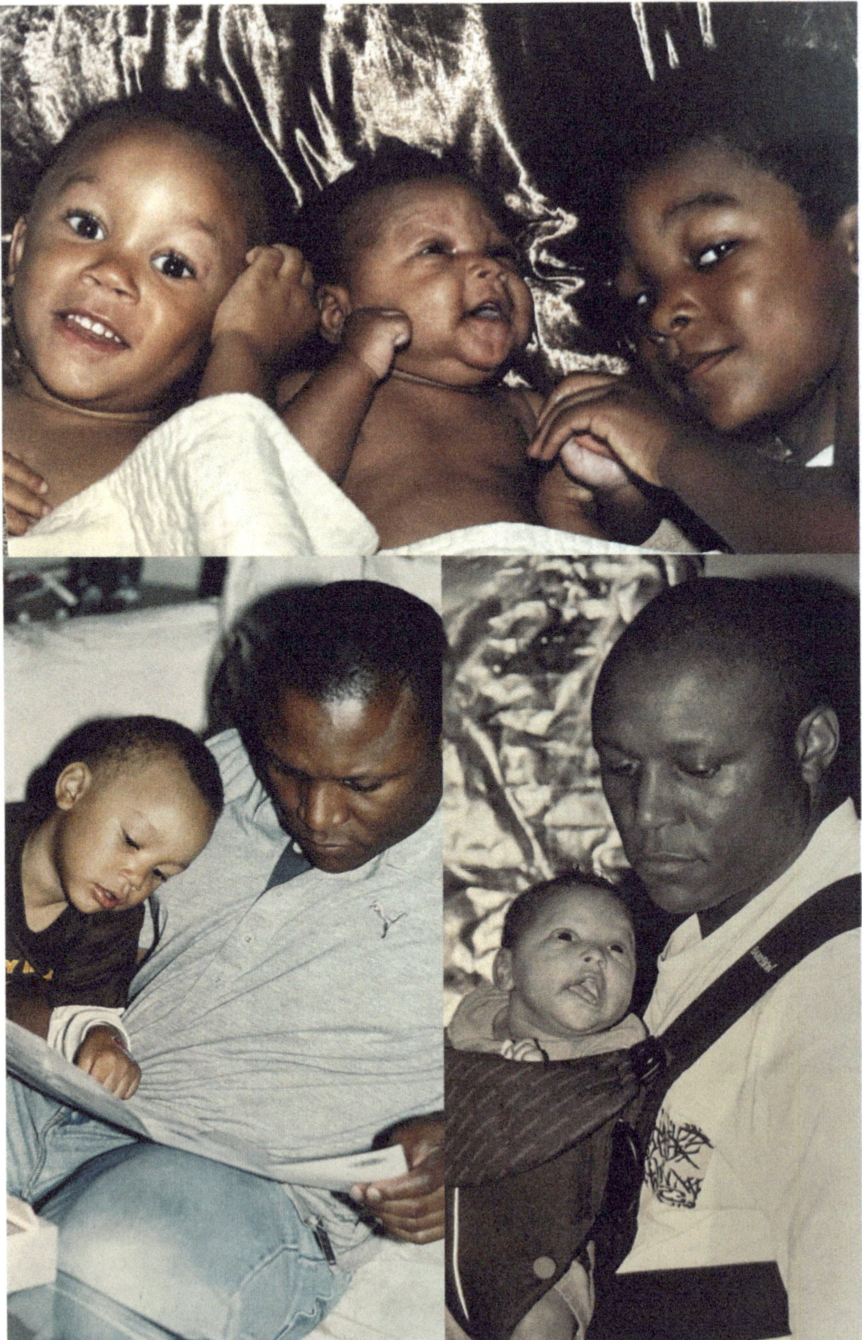

Top: Barry Sanders' three youngest sons Nigel, Nic and Noah are shown waiting for their brother, B.J. to visit. **Above left:** Barry Sanders is shown with his son Nic, while reading toy assembly directions. **Above right:** Barry Sanders is shown with baby Noah, who loved being carried.

Left: Barry Sanders is shown reading to his son, Nigel. **Middle:** Pictured are members of Barry Sanders' family in front of the Barry Sanders statue outside of Boone Pickens stadium in Stillwater. **Bottom:** Pictured are Barry Sanders and family members Diane, Ellisa, Donna, B.J., Aaron, Nia, Nigel, Gloria, Nicholas, Elaine, Noah and Lydell at the grand opening of the Barry Sanders Nissan car dealership.

Top: Barry Sanders is shown with his sons, Noah, B.J., Nigel and Nic during the grand opening of the Barry Sanders Nissan car dealership. **Above left:** Barry Sanders is shown with his oldest son, B.J., after one of B.J.'s football games at Oklahoma State. **Above right:** Barry Sanders is shown with, Noah, Ellisa, B.J., Nicholas, Myles and Krista, while hanging out in Michigan the week of Nic's high school graduation. **Right:** Barry Sanders is shown with his sisters, from left, Donna, Elissa, Krista and Gina with the Heisman Trophy.

Left: Barry Sanders is shown with his oldest son, B.J. in Wichita, KS. **Middle left:** Barry Sanders is shown with Tollie Sanders, Sr., his paternal grandfather, front yard of grandfather's home. **Middle right:** Barry Sanders is shown with his son, Nigel, not long after he was born. **Bottom:** Barry Sanders is shown with family at Disney World in Florida.

Above: Barry Sanders is shown with lifelong friend Mark McCormick and Mark's nephew Shaun Pannell. **Right:** Barry Sanders is shown with his son, Nigel. **Below:** Barry Sanders is shown holding his son, Noah, while vacationing at Sea Island.

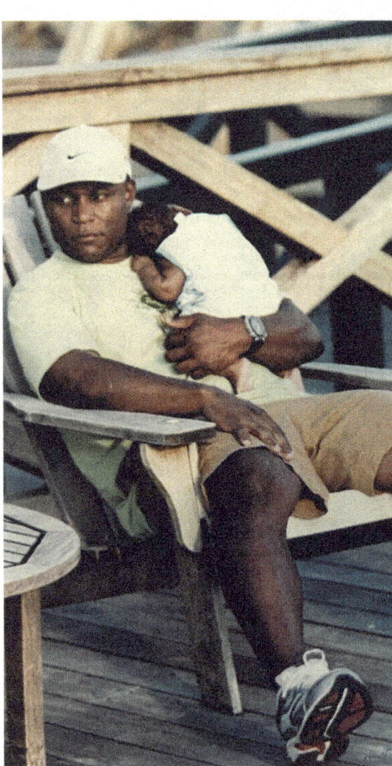

AN INVITATION

From Barry Sanders

I hope you enjoyed this book. I hope it gave you some insight into my story and my life. I enjoyed working on this and sharing with you.

We have a lot of giveaways and more photos and videos of my life on my website. Please stop by!

If you'd like to connect with me, please check out my website:

barrysanders.com

You can also connect with me on social media:

TikTok: tiktok.com/@barrysandersreal

Facebook: facebook.com/BarrySanders Official/

Twitter: twitter.com/BarrySanders

Instagram: instagram.com/barrysanders/

APPENDIX

Barry Sanders

Barry Sanders played in the National Football League for the Detroit Lions from 1989-98, where he had a groundbreaking career as a running back. He was the Most Valuable Player in 1991 and 1997, and became a Pro Football Hall of Fame member in 2004. He is a businessman, father and fan. Before his storied career in the NFL, he won the Heisman Trophy in 1988, during his college career at Oklahoma State University.

Barry's journey is filled with athletic achievement, humility and respect for his family, teammates and fans alike. Barry's triumphs against the odds undeniably reflects the power of personal perseverance and commitment. The integrity that runs rock-solid through his career is a lifelong embodiment of the heart and strength he witnessed in his mother's resolve and his sister Nancy's life, a value system he carries forth in his faith still today.

What's most remarkable is how his background prepared him for and culminated in one of the most storied careers in NFL history. In heartfelt words, dazzling photos and rare video, he shares the story of his life with you.

Pictured, from left, are Barry's lifelong friend Mark McCormick, Barry's agent J.B. Bernstein and Barry Sanders.

Mark E. McCormick

Mark E. McCormick is Barry's lifelong friend, a former columnist for The Wichita Eagle, current columnist for The Kansas Reflector, and is now the Deputy Executive Director for Special Initiatives at ACLU of Kansas. He has also been appointed to the Kansas African American Affairs Commission as a board chairman and to the Commission on Racial Equality and Justice by Kansas Gov. Laura Kelly.

Mark has been featured in various publications and films, has won many awards and is the trustee at The University of Kansas, his alma mater, where he is involved in the school of Journalism. He has more than 20 years journalism experience as a reporter, editor and columnist, and is a New York Times bestselling author.

Mark McCormick, shown right, is with his journalism professor from the University of Kansas, Susanne Shaw.

Made in the USA
Monee, IL
19 December 2023